THE WORKS OF MISS HAVERGAL.

DEVOTIONAL.

THE ROYAL INVITATION; or, Daily Thoughts on Coming to Christ. LOYAL RESPONSES; or, Daily Melodies for the King's Minstrels. 18mo. Cloth, red edges, **75** cts.

Either of the above, in separate volumes.
Cloth, white edge, each, **25** cts.

ROYAL COMMANDMENTS; or, Morning Thoughts for the King's Servants. ROYAL BOUNTY; or, Evening Thoughts for the King's Guests. 18mo. Cloth, **75** cts.

Either of the above in separate volumes.
Cloth, white edge, each, **25** cts.

MY KING; or, Daily Thoughts for the King's Children. 18mo. Cloth, red edge, **50** cts.
Cloth, white edge, **25** cts.

The beauty and purpose of this little volume are of the very highest and comfort has an abiding place in every page.

KEPT FOR THE MASTER'S USE. Cloth, red edge, ink and gold stamp, **50** cts.
Cloth, white edge, **25** cts.;

In this volume the author enforces the great lesson of consecration which she learned so well, and illustrated so perfectly by her earnest spirit and tireless activity.

RED LETTER DAYS. Cloth, red edge, **85** cts.

A collection of texts and verses, with corresponding blank pages for birthday and other records, for every day in the year.

ECHOES FROM THE WORD FOR THE CHRISTIAN YEAR. With Prefatory Note, by Rev. Charles Bullock. Cloth, white edge, **40** cts.

Either or all of the above sent by mail, postage paid, on receipt of the price. Fractional amounts can be remitted in postage stamps.

ANSON D. F. RANDOLPH & CO.,

900 *Broadway, cor. 20th St., New York.*

MY KING;

OR,

DAILY THOUGHTS FOR THE KING'S CHILDREN.

BY

FRANCES RIDLEY HAVERGAL.

"My King and my God!"—Ps. v. 2.

TWELFTH THOUSAND.

NEW YORK:
ANSON D. F. RANDOLPH & COMPANY,
900 BROADWAY, COR. 20th STREET.

PREFATORY NOTE.

THE number of beautiful texts and topics "touching the King" is far too large for the plan of this little book. The difficulty lay in selection.

None but Old Testament texts, chiefly typical ones, have been taken for the daily portions; and the wide, bright fields of the future—the coming glory and reign of our King—have been left untouched. Only those passages have been chosen which concern the actual present reign of Christ our King, and the practical present life of His true subjects. And still there are too many! The Throne, the Palace, the Royal Bounty, the Wisdom, the

Favor of the King, and many other points, will give pleasant opportunity to earnest readers for further search and study.

It is my happy hope and prayer that these simple "Daily Thoughts" may quicken the glad loyalty and loving praise of some of His children, and that the blessing of my King may go forth with *every* copy. "Let the children of Zion be joyful in their King," and then "Daily shall HE be praised!"

F. R. H.

December 5, 1876.

CONTENTS.

For Sundays.

FIRST DAY.

The Source of the Kingship.

"Because the Lord hath loved His people, He hath made thee king over them." 2 Chron. ii. 11; ix. 8.

CHRIST said to His Father, "Thou lovedst me before the foundation of the world." John xvii. 24. At that mysterious date, not of time, but of everlasting love, God "chose us in Him." Eph. i. 4. Before the world began, God, that can not lie, Titus i. 2. gave the promise of eternal life to Him for us, and made with Him for us "a covenant ordered in all things, and sure." 2 Sam. xxiii. 5 The leading provisions of that covenant were, a Lamb for our atonement and a King for our government—a dying and a living Saviour. This God the Father did for us, and His own divine interest is strongly indicated in the

typical words, "God will provide *Himself* a
Gen. xxii. 8. Lamb," and "I have provided *me* a
1 Sam. xvi. 1. King." So the Source of the Kingship of Christ is God Himself, in the eternal
counsels of His love. It is one of the grand
Ps. cxxxix. 17 "thoughts of God."

Having provided, He appointed
and anointed His King: "Yet have I set (mar-
Ps. ii. 6. gin, anointed) my King upon my
holy hill of Zion." What a marvelous
meeting-place is thus found in the Kingship of
Jesus for God's heart and ours! He says in
His majestic sovereignty, "I have set *my* King;"
and we say, in lowly and loving loyalty, "Thou
Ps. xliv. 4. art *my* King."

God has appointed His King "to
1 Kings i. 35. be ruler over Israel *and* over Judah."
Thus He gives His children a great
bond of union. For "one King shall be King
Ezek. xxxvii. 22. to them all," and He shall "gather
together in one the children of God
John xi. 52. which were scattered abroad." "Satan scatters, but Jesus gathers." Shall
we then let the enemy have his way, and induce
us to keep apart and aloof from those over whom

our beloved King reigns also? Let us try this day to recollect this, and make it practical in all our contact with His other subjects.

Why has God made Jesus King? Who would have guessed the right answer? "*Because* the Lord loved His people." So the very thought of the Kingship of Christ sprang from the everlasting love of God to His people. Bring that wonderful statement down to personal reality—"His people"—that is, *you* and *me*. God made Jesus King over you because He loved you, and that with nothing less than the love wherewith He loved Him. Which is the more wonderful—the love that devised such a gift, or the gift that was devised by such love! Oh, to realize the glorious value of it! May we, who by His grace know something of God's gift of His Son as our Saviour, learn day by day more of the magnificent preciousness of His gift of His Anointed One as our King!

Jer. xxxi. 3.

John xvii. 26.

SECOND DAY.

The Promise of the King.

Hos. xiii. 10. "I will be thy King."

HE knows our need of a king. He knows
the hopeless anarchy, not only of a
Ib. iii. 4. world, but of a heart, "without a
king." Is there a more desolate
Ib. x. 3. cry than, "We have no king?"—
none to reverence and love, none to
obey, none to guide and protect us and rule
over us, none to keep us in that truest freedom
of whole-hearted loyalty. Have we not felt
Isa. lvii. 10, 18. that we really want a strong hand
over our hearts? that having our
own way is not so good as another's way, if
only that other is one to whom our hearty and
entire confidence and allegiance can be and
are given? Has there not been an echo in
our souls of the old cry, "Give me a king?'

—a cry that nothing can still but this Divine promise, "*I* will be thy King!" Hos. xiii. 10.

But the promise has been given; and now, if the old desolate wail of a kingless heart comes up in an hour of faithless forgetfulness, His word comes like a royal clarion, "Now, *why* dost thou cry out aloud? Mic. iv. 9.
Is there no king in thee?" And then the King's gracious assurance falls with hushing power, "I will be *thy* King."

How glad we are that He Himself is our King! For we are so sure that He Phil. iii. 21.
is able even to subdue all things unto Himself in this inner kingdom Mic. vii. 19.
which we can not govern at all. We are so glad to take Him at His Rom. vii. 19.
word, and give up the government into His hands, asking Him to be our King in very deed, and to set up His throne of peace in the long-disturbed and divided citadel, praying that He would bring every 2 Cor. x. 5.
thought into captivity to His gentle obedience.

We have had enough of revolutions and revolts, of tyrants and traitors, of lawlessness

and of self-framed codes. Other lords (and
Isa. xxvi. 13. oh, how many!) have had domin-
ion over us. He has permitted us to
be their servants, that now, by blessed and rest-
2 Chron. xii. 8. ful contrast, we may know His service. Now we *only* want "another
Acts xvii. 7. King, one Jesus." He has made us
willing in the day of His power,
Ps. cx. 3. and that was the first act of His
reign, and the token that "of the
Isa. ix. 7. *increase* of His government and
peace there shall be no end" in our
hearts.

Lord, be Thou my King this day! Reign more absolutely in me than ever before. Let the increase of Thy government be continual
2 Thess. i. 12. and mighty in me, so that Thy
name may be glorified in me now
and forever.

Reign over me, Lord Jesus!
  Oh, make my heart Thy throne!
It shall be Thine forever,
  It shall be Thine alone!

THIRD DAY.

Allegiance to the King.

"Thou art my King." Ps. xliv. 4.

FIRST, *can* I say it?

Is Jesus in very deed and truth "my King?" Where is the proof of it? Am I living in His kingdom of "righteousness and peace and joy in the Holy Ghost" now? Rom. xiv. 17. Am I speaking the language of that kingdom? Am I following "the customs of the people" which are not His people? Jer. x 3. or do I "diligently learn the ways of His people?" Ib. xii. 16. Am I practically living under the rule of His laws? Have I done heart homage to Him? Am I bravely and honestly upholding His cause because it is His, not merely because those around me do so? Is my allegiance making any practical difference to my life to-day?

Next, *ought* I to say it?

What! any question about that? The King
Acts xx. 28. who came Himself to purchase me
from my tyrant and His foe; the
King, who laid aside His crown and His royal
Phil. ii. 7. robes and left His kingly palace and
came down Himself to save a rebel;
the King, who, though He was rich, yet for my
sake became poor, that I "through His pov-
2 Cor. viii. 9. erty might be rich"—*ought* I to acknowledge Him? Is it a question
1 Thess. ii. 12. of "*ought* I?" God has "called me
unto His kingdom and glory;" He
Col. i. 13. "hath translated me into the kingdom of the Son of His love;" and
shall the loyal words falter or fail from my lips,
"Thou art my King?"

Lastly, *do* I say it?

Ps. xlv. 11. God has said to me, "He *is* thy
Lord and worship thou Him." Do
John xx. 28. my lips say, "My Lord and my
God?" Does my life say, "Christ
Phil. iii. 8. Jesus, *my* Lord"—definitely and
personally, "*my* Lord?" Can I
share in His last sweet commendation to His

disciples, the more precious because of its divine dignity, "Ye call me Master John xiii. 13.
and Lord, *and ye say well*, for so I am?" Have I said, "Thou *art my* Ps. lxxxi. 15, mar.
King" to Jesus Himself, from the depth of my own heart in unreserved and unfeigned submission to His sceptre? Am I ashamed or afraid to confess my al- Matt. x. 32.
legiance in plain English among His friends or before His foes? Is the seal upon my brow so unmistakable that always and everywhere I am known to be His subject? Is "Thou art my King" blazoned, Acts iv. 13.
as it ought to be, in shining letters on the whole scroll of my life, so that 2 Cor. iii. 2.
it may be "known and read of all men?"

Answer Thou for me, O my King! "Search me and try me," and show me the Ps. cxxxix. 23.
true state of my case, and then for Thine own sake pardon all my past Ib. xxv. 11.
disloyalty, and make me by Thy mighty grace from this moment totally loyal! For "Thou *art* my King!'

FOURTH DAY.

Decision for the King.

2 Sam. iii. 17, 18. "Ye sought for David in times past to be king over you. Now, then, do it."

Ib. v. 2. "IN time past, when Saül was king over us, thou wast he that leddest out and broughtest in Israel."
Ps. lxxxix. 19, 20. Chosen, anointed, given by God, continually leading and caring for
Isa. lv. 4. us, yet not accepted, not crowned, not enthroned by us; our real al-
Rom. vi. 16. legiance, our actual service given to another! Self has been our Saul,
Ib. vii. 23. our central tyranny; and many have been its officers domineering in every department.

"Ye sought for David in times past to be king over you." Well we might, for the bond-
Isa. xiv. 3. age of any other lord was daily harder. Well we might, with even

a dim glimpse of the grace and glory of the
King who waited for our homage. We sought,
first, only for something—we hardly knew what
—restlessly and vaguely; then, for some One,
who was not merely "the Desire of Hag. ii. 7.
all nations," but our own desire.
And yet we did not come to the 1 Kings xviii.
point; we were not ready for His 21.
absolute monarchy, for we were loving and doing the will of our old tyrant.

But "the time past of our life 1 Pet. iv. 3.
may suffice us to have wrought the
will" of self—Satan—the world. We do not
want "to live the rest of our time" Ib. iv. 2.
to any but One Will. We come face
to face with a great NOW! "Now, 2 Sam. iii. 18.
then, do it!" "Now, then," let us,
with full purpose of heart, dethrone the usurper
and give the diadem to Him "whose Ezek. xxi. 26
right it is," a blood-bought and 27.
death-sealed right.

He does not force allegiance—He waits for
it. The crown of our own individ- 2 Sam. v. 3.
ual love and loyalty must be offered
by our own hands. We must "do it." When?

Oh, now! *Now* let us come to Jesus as our King. *Now* let us, first in solemn, heart-surrender, and then in open and unmistakable life-confession, yield ourselves to Him as our Sovereign, our Ruler.

What a glorious life of victory and peace opens before us when this is done! What a silencing of our fears lest the time to come should nevertheless be as the time past!
2 Sam. iii. 18. "Now, then, do it: FOR the Lord hath spoken of David, saying, By the hand of my servant David I will save my people Israel out of the hand of the Philistines, and out of the hand of all their enemies."

Rev. xxii. 19. Now, do not let us "take away from the words" of this promise, and merely hope that our King *may* save us from *some* of our enemies. The Lord hath said, "*will* save from *all*." Let us trust our true David this day to fulfill the word of the Lord, and verily we shall not fail to find that
Matt. ix. 29. according to our faith it shall be unto us.

FIFTH DAY.

The First to Meet the King.

"For thy servant doth know that I have sinned; therefore, behold, I am come the first this day of all the house of Joseph to meet my lord the king." 2 Sam. xix. 20.

YES, I have sinned. I *know* that I have sinned. Whether I feel it more or less does not touch the fact: I *know* it. And what then? "THEREFORE, behold, I am come the first this day of all . . . . to meet my lord the King."

Just because I *know* that I have sinned, I come to Jesus. He came to call sinners. He came to save sinners, so He came to call and to save me. "This is all my desire." Matt. ix. 13. 1 Tim. i. 15. 2 Sam. xxiii 5.

Just because I know that *I* have

sinned, I may and must come "the first of all." Thousands are coming, but the heart
Prov. xiv. 10. knoweth his own bitterness. So,
not waiting for others, not coming in order, but "first of all," by the pressure of my sore need of pardon, I come. There is no waiting for one's turn in coming to Jesus.

"The first of all," because it is against "*my* lord the King" that I have sinned. I am His
Ps. cxvi. 16. servant, so I have the greater sin.
"The first of all," because I have so
Luke vii. 47. much to be forgiven, and have already been forgiven so much, that I
Col. ii. 13. must, I do, love much; and love,
even of a sorrowing sinner, seeks nearness, and can not rest in distance.

"Therefore," also, "I am come *this day*.'
I dare not and could not wait till to-
Matt. xx. 30. morrow. No need to wait, even till
to-night! Now! He is passing by,
2 Sam. xix. 16. and I must "haste to meet" Him.
Isa. lv. 6. "While He is near," I will tell Him all.

Zech. ix. 9. I am come to *meet* Him, not merely to *go* to Him; for He is always com-

ing to meet us. He was on His way Luke xv. 18.
before I had said, "I will arise and
go." I come, because He comes to me.

Yet I could not come with this terrible knowledge that I have sinned, but that I know something more. I know that He hath said,
"Come unto me." I know that He Matt. xi. 28.
hath said, "Him that cometh I will
in nowise cast out." This is enough; John vi. 37.
therefore I am come to my Lord the
King.

Not to His servants, but to Him- Matt. xv. 23.
self. Even those who stand near 2 Sam. xix.
Him may accuse and condemn, but 21.
the King Himself will receive me Hos. xiv. 2.
graciously; for, with Him, there is
forgiveness and mercy and plente- Ps. cxxx. 4, 7.
ous redemption.

And though the oath of an earthly sovereign may be broken, my King (in 1 Kings ii. 8.
glorious contrast to the imperfect 9.
human type) "keepeth His promise Ps. cxlvi. 5.
forever." His covenant will He not (P. B. V.)
break, nor alter the thing that is Ps. lxxxix.
gone out of His lips. Therefore, 34

1 John ii. 25. the eternal life which He hath promised me is secured to me forever;
John x. 28. for He hath said, "I give unto them
eternal life, and they shall never per-
ish, neither shall any man pluck them out of my hand."

SIXTH DAY.

The Condescension of the King.

"Behold, thy King cometh unto thee." Zech. ix. 9.

THAT our King should let us come to Him is condescension indeed. But have we praised Him for His still more wonderful condescension: "Thy King *cometh unto thee?*" "Unto *thee*," rebel, traitor, faithless subject, coward, and cold-hearted follower; for where is the life that has not fallen under these charges when seen in the double light of the King's perfect law and the King's great love? Yes, He cometh unto *thee*, and it is enough to break our hearts when we get one contrasted glimpse of this undeserved grace and unparalleled condescension. Isa. xlviii. 8.

His great promise has had its first fulfillment "unto thee." It is a finished fact of sevenfold grace. Thy King has come, and His own voice

has given the objects of His coming—“to do
Heb. x. 9. Matt. v. 17. Thy will, O God;” “to fulfill” the
Ib. ix. 13. law; “to call sinners to repent-
Luke xix. 10. ance;” “to seek and to save that
John x. 10. which was lost;” “that they might
have life, and that they might have it more
Ib. xii. 46. abundantly;” “a light into the world
that whosoever believeth on me
should not abide in darkness.” What He came
Ib. xvii. 4. to do He has done, for “He faileth
Zeph. iii. 5. not.” On this we may and ought to
Isa. xliv. 23. rest quietly and undoubtingly, for
“the Lord hath *done* it.”

But you want a further fulfillment—you want
Cant. iii. 1. a present coming of your King.
You have His most sweet word, “I
John xiv. 18. will come to you;” and you re-
Ps. ci. 2. spond, “Oh, *when* wilt Thou come
unto me?” Are you ready to receive the
Ib. cxliii. 6. King's own answer now? Do you
so desire His coming that you do
not want it postponed at all? Can you defer
Ib. lxxiii. 25. all other comers and say in reality,
Cant. iv. 16. “*Let* my Beloved come?”

He has but one answer to that appeal

Hush! listen! believe! for the King speaks to
you: "I am come into my garden, Cant. v. 1.
my sister, my spouse." He *is* come.
Do not miss the unspeakable blessing and joy
of meeting Him and resting in His Ib. ii. 3.
presence by hurrying away to anything else, by listening to any outward call.
Stay *now*, lay the little book aside, kneel down
at your King's feet, doubt not His word, which
is "more sure" than even the "ex- 2 Pet. i. 19.
cellent glory" that apostles beheld,
and thank Him for coming to you. 1 Kings x. 2.
Commune with Him now of all that
is in your heart, and "rejoice greatly;" for
"behold, thy King cometh unto thee."

"Jesus comes to hearts rejoicing,
Bringing news of sin forgiven;
Jesus comes in sounds of gladness,
Leading souls redeemed to heaven.

"Jesus comes again in mercy,
When our hearts are bowed with care;
Jesus comes again in answer
To an earnest heartfelt prayer."

—GODFREY THRING.

SEVENTH DAY.

The Indwelling of the King.

Jer. viii. 19. "Is not her King in her?"

WAITING for a royal coming—what expectation, what preparation, what tension! A glimpse for many, a full view for some, a word for a favored few, and the pageant is over like a dream. The Sovereign may come, but does not stay.

Our King comes not thus: He comes not
Zech. ii. 10. to pass, but to "*dwell* in the midst
2 Cor. vi. 16. of thee;" not only in His Church
collectively, but in each believer individually.
Luke xxiv. 29. We pray, "Abide with us," and He
answers in the sublime plural of God-
John xiv. 23. head, "We will come unto him, and
make our abode with him." Even
this grand abiding with us does not extend to

the full marvels of His condescension and His nearness, for the next time He speaks of it He changes the "with" to "in," and thenceforth only speaks of "I *in* you," "I in him," "I in them." John xv. 4, 5. John xvii. 23.

Now do not let us say, "How can this be?" but, like Mary, "How shall this be?" The means, though not the mode, of the mystery is revealed for our grasp of adoring wonder: "That Christ may dwell in your heart by faith." It is almost too wonderful to dare to speak of. Christ Himself, my King, coming to me, into me! abiding, dwelling in my very heart! Really staying there all day, all night, wherever I am, whatever I am doing; here in my poor unworthy heart at this very moment! And this only because the grace that flowed from His own love has broken the bars of doubt, and because He has given the faith that wanted Him and welcomed Him. Let us pause a little to take it in! John iii. 9. Luke i. 34. Eph. iii. 17. Jer. xxxi. 3. Eph. ii. 8.

The more we have known of the plague of our own heart, the more inconceivably wonderful this indwelling of 1 Kings viii. 38.

Christ will appear—much more wonderful than
Luke ii. 7. that He chose a manger as His royal
resting-place, for that had never
been defiled by sin, and had never harbored
His enemy. It is no use trying to comprehend
this incomprehensible grace of our King—we
have only to believe His promise, saying,
1 Kings i. 36. "Amen; the Lord God of my Lord
the King say so too."

There should be three practical results of
this belief:—1. *Holiness.* We must see to it
Eph. iv. 31. that we resolutely "put away" all
1 Cor. iii. 16, 17. that ought not to be in His royal
2 Cor. vii. 1. abode. "Having, therefore, these
promises, dearly beloved, let us cleanse ourselves from *all* filthiness of the flesh and spirit,
perfecting holiness in the fear of God." 2. *Confidence.* What does the citadel fear when an
invincible general is within it? "The Lord
Zeph. iii. 17. thy God in the midst of thee is
mighty; He will save." He is
Zech. ii. 5. "the wall of fire round about," and
"the glory in the midst of her;" and "he that
Ib. ii. 8. toucheth you toucheth the apple of
Zeph. iii. 14. His eye." 3. *Joy.* Yes! "Be glad

and rejoice with all the heart," "sing and rejoice, O daughter of Zion; for, lo, I
come, and I will dwell in the midst
of thee, saith the Lord." Zech. ii. 10.

EIGHTH DAY.

Full Satisfaction in the King.

2 Sam. xix. 30. "Yea, let him take all, forasmuch as my lord the king is come again in peace to his own house."

IT is when the King has really come in peace to His own home in the "contrite
Isa. lvii. 15. and humble spirit" (not before)—
John xiv. 23. when He has entered in to make His abode there (not before)—that the soul is satis-
Ps. xxii. 26. fied with Him alone, and is ready to let any Ziba take all else, because all else really seems nothing at all in comparison to
Matt. xiii. 46. the conscious possession of the Treasure of treasures.

Isa. xxxiii. 6. Sometimes this is reached at once, in the first flush of wondering joy at finding the King really "come in peace" to the empty soul which wanted to be "His own

house." Sometimes very gradually Heb. iii. 6.
—as year after year we realize His indwelling more and more, and find again and again that He is quite enough to satisfy us in all circumstances; that the empty corners of the " house " are filled one after another; that the old longings have somehow gone Ps. iv. 6.
away, and the old ambitions van- Cf. Eccles. and Cant.
ished; that the old tastes and interests in the things of the world are superseded by stronger tastes and interests in the things of Christ; that He is day by day Eph. i. 23.
more really *filling* our lives—we Phil. iii. 8.
" count " (because we really find) one thing after another " but loss for the excellency of the knowledge of Christ Jesus my Lord," till He leads us on to the rapturous joy of the " Yea, doubtless," and "*all* things! "

Now, have we got as far as saying "*some* things," without being quite sure about "*all* things? " Do you see that it all hinges upon Jesus coming into the heart as " His *own* house " —*altogether* " His own? " For if Acts xxvi. 29.
there are some rooms of which we do not give up the key—some little sitting-room

which we would like to keep as a little mental retreat, with a view from the window, which we do not quite want to give up—some lodger whom we would rather not send away just yet—some little dark closet which we have not resolution to open and set to rights—of course the King has not full possession; it is not all and really "His own;" and the very misgiving about it proves that He has *therefore* not yet "come again in peace." It is no use expecting
Isa. xxvi. 3. "perfect peace," while He has a
Mic. vi. 2. secret controversy with us about
Acts v. 2. any withholding of what is "His
own" by purchase. Only throw open *all* the
Rev. iii. 20. doors, "and the King of Glory shall
Ps. xxiv. 9. come in," and then there will be no
Hag. ii. 7. craving for other guests. He will "fill
this house with glory," and there will be no place left for gloom.

Is it not so? Bear witness, tell it out, you with whom the King dwells in peace! Life is filled with bright interests, time is filled with happy work or peaceful waiting, the mind is filled with His beautiful words and thoughts, the heart is filled with His presence, and you "abide satisfied" with Him! Yes, "tell it out!" Prov. xix. 23.

The human heart asks love; but now I know
That my heart hath from Thee
All real, and full, and marvelous affection,
So near, so human! yet Divine perfection
Thrills gloriously the mighty glow!
Thy love is enough for me!

There were strange soul-depths, restless, vast, and broad,
Unfathomed as the sea;
An infinite craving for some infinite stilling;
But now Thy perfect love is perfect filling!
Lord Jesus Christ, my Lord, my God,
Thou, Thou art enough for me.

NINTH DAY.

The Sorrow of the King.

2 Sam. xv. 23. "The king himself also passed over the brook Kidron." *

John xviii. 1 "JESUS went forth with His disciples over the brook Cedron."† How precisely the Old Testament shadow corresponds with the New Testament fulfillment! The king, in sorrow and humiliation, is here brought before us, passing from his royal home, from all his glory and gladness

2 Sam. xviii. 20. —passing over into exile and unknown distresses.

There is no need for imagination in dwelling on His sorrows. The pathos of the plain words is more than enough; no pen has power to add to it. Let us listen to them just as they

---

* Kidron means "obscurity;" † Cedron is "black" or "sad."

stand—not hurrying over them because they are only texts, and we know them all beforehand; they are the Holy Ghost's sevenfold testimony to the sorrow of the King.

"A man of sorrows and ac- Isa. liii. 3.
quainted with grief." "I am poor Ps. lxix. 29.
and sorrowful." "The sorrows of Ps. xviii. 4, 5.
death compassed me." "The sor-
rows of hell compassed me." "Be- Lam. i. 12.
hold and see if there be any sorrow
like unto my sorrow." "He began Matt. xxvi.
to be sorrowful and very heavy." 37.
"My soul is exceeding sorrowful, Ib. xxvi. 38.
even unto death." Oh, stay a little
that you may take it in! Hear Jesus saying to
you, "Hear, I pray you, and be- Lam. i. 18.
hold my sorrow!"

"Surely He hath borne our griefs Isa. liii. 4.
and carried our sorrows." The sorrows of the past, the very sorrow that may be pressing heavily at this moment; all yours, all mine; all the sorrows of all His children all through the groaning generations; all that were "too heavy" for them—Jesus bore Ps. xxxviii. 4
them all. "Is it nothing to you?" Lam. i. 12.

It is when the Lord says, "Now will I gather them (the rebels and wanderers), that He adds,
Hos. viii. 10. "And they shall sorrow a little for the burden of the King of princes."
Have we this proof that He has indeed gath-
2 Sam. xv. 23. ered us? For "*all* the people," except the rebels, "passed over with the king." Do we know anything of this passage over Cedron, the brook of sadness, with Him? Possibly it seems presumptuous to
Phil. iii. 10. think of sharing "the fellowship of His sufferings," that mysterious privilege! But mark, it was not only the mighty Ittai and "all his men," the nobles and the veterans, that passed over, but "all
2 Sam. xv. 22. the little ones that were with him," too. And so "the little ones, the
1 Cor. xii. 26, 27. weak ones," the least member of His body may thus "continue
Luke xxii. 28. with" Jesus; and nothing brings one closer to another than a shared sorrow.

But look forward! Because He has drunk
Ps. cx. 7. "of the brook in the way, therefore shall He lift up the head." Already

the "exceeding sorrowful" is exchanged for "Thou hast made Him (the King) exceeding glad;" and when the ransomed and gathered of the Lord shall return with everlasting joy, "their King also shall pass before them."

Matt. xxvi. 38. Ps. xxi. 6. Isa. xxxv. 10 Mic. ii. 13.

TENTH DAY.

Going Forth with the King.

Sam. xix. 25. "The king said, Wherefore wentest thou not with me?"

John xvii. 24. "WITH me!" To be with our King will be our highest bliss for eternity; and surely it
1 Thess. iv. 17. is the position of highest honor and gladness now. But if we would always *be* with Him, we must sometimes be ready to *go* with Him.

"The Son of God goes forth to war" nowadays. Do we go with Him? His cross is "without the gate." Do we go "forth unto
Heb. xiii. 12, 13. Him without the camp, bearing His reproach?" Do we really go with Him every day and all day long, following
Rev. xiv. 4. "the Lamb whithersoever He goeth?" What about this week—this

day? Have we loyally gone with our King wherever His banner, His footsteps, go before? 1 Pet. ii. 21.

If the voice of our King is heard in our hearts, "Wherefore wentest *thou* not with me"—thou who hast eaten "continually at the King's table"—thou who hast had a place among "the King's sons"—thou unto whom the King has shown "the kindness of God," we have no "because" to offer. He would have healed the spiritual lameness that hindered, and we might have run after Him. We are without excuse. 2 Sam. ix. 13. Ib. ix. 11. Ib. ix. 3. 2 Sam. xix. 26. Cant. i. 4.

It is only now that we can go with Jesus into conflict, suffering, loneliness, weariness. It is only now that we can come to the help of the Lord against the mighty in this great battle-field. Shall we shrink from opportunities which are not given to the angels? Surely, even with Him in glory, the disciples must "remember the words of the Lord Jesus, how He said" to them, "Ye are they which have continued Judges v. 23. Luke xi. 23. Acts xx. 35. Luke xxii. 28

with me in my temptations," with a thrill of rapturous thanksgiving that such a privilege was theirs.

There will be no more suffering with Him in
2 Tim. ii. 12. heaven, only reigning with Him; no more fighting under His banner,
Rev. iii. 21. only sitting with Him on His throne. But to-day we may prove our loving and grateful allegiance to our King in the presence of His enemies by rising up and going forth with Him—forth *from* a life of easy idleness or selfish business—forth *into* whatever form of blessed fellowship in His work, His
2 Cor. vi. 1. wars, or, it may be, of His sufferings,
Phil. iii. 10. the King Himself may choose for us. We have heard His call, "Come *unto* me."
Cant. iv. 8. To-day He says, "Come *with* me."

True-hearted, whole-hearted; Faithful and loyal,
 King of our lives, by Thy grace we will be!
Under Thy standard exalted and royal,
 Strong in Thy strength we will battle for Thee!

ELEVENTH DAY.

The Smiting of the King.

"I will smite the king only." 2 Sam. xvii. 2

IT may be that this futile threat of a wicked man against the king was like the saying of Caiaphas—"not of himself," but John xi. 51. written for our learning "more about Rom. xv. 4. Jesus." A deadly stroke was to be aimed at "the king only," for he was "worth Cf. 1 Kings xxii. 31. ten thousand" of the people; if he 2 Sam. xviii. 3 were smitten, they should escape. Do the words of David in another place tell of his great Antitype's desire that it should be so? "Let Thine hand, I pray Thee, O 1 Chron. xxi. 17. Lord my God, be on me, ... but NOT on Thy people." "For the Isa. liii. 8. transgression of my people was the stroke upon Him" (*margin*); therefore not upon us, never upon us. The lightning that strikes the conductor instead of the building to which it is joined, has spent its fiery force and strikes no more.

Not the hand of an impotent foe, but the sharp sword of the omnipotent Lord of hosts,
Zech. xiii. 7. was lifted to smite His Shepherd—
Heb. xiii. 20. our Shepherd-king, The Great, The
1 Pet. v. 4. Chief, The Good (and the Beautiful,
John x. 11. as the original implies). Think of
Isa. liii. 4. the words, "stricken, smitten of
1 Pet. i. 8. God," with their unknown depths of
agony, and then of Jesus, Him whom we love, fathoming those black depths of agony *alone!*
Isa. lxiii. 3. "*Jesus smitten of God!*" can we
even *say* the words, and not feel moved as no other grief could move us? Do not let us shrink from dwelling upon it; let us rather ask the Holy Spirit, even now, to show us a little of what this awful smiting really was —to show us our dear Lord Jesus Christ, in
John xv. 13. this tremendous proving of His own
Rom. v. 8. and His Father's love—to whisper
in our hearts as we gaze upon the Crucified
John xix. 14. One, "Behold *your* King!"

"The King *only*." For "by Himself He

purged our sins." Certainly we had nothing to do with it then! certainly no other man or means had anything to do with it! and certainly nothing and no one now can touch that great fact, so far out of reach of human quibbling and meddling, that Jesus "His own self, bare our sins in His own body on the tree." Is not the fact that He "with whom we have to do" *was smitten of God instead of us*, enough? What else can we want to guarantee our salvation?

Heb. i. 3.

1 Pet. ii. 24.

Heb. iv. 13.

"The King *only*." For the sorrow of our King is shared with His people; but in the smiting we have no part. We can only stand "afar off," bowed and hushed in shuddering love, as the echoes of the awful stripes that fell on Him float down through the listening centuries, while each throb of the healed heart replies, "For me! for me!"

Matt. xxvii. 55.

Isa. liii. 5.

"I have trodden the wine-press *alone*, and of the people there was none with me."

Isa. lxiii. 3.

TWELFTH DAY.

The Kinship of the King.

2 Sam. xix. 42. "The king is near of kin to us."

NOT only in the Prophet raised up "from
the midst of thee, of thy brethren," and
Deut. xviii. 15. in the High-Priest, "thy brother,"
Ex. xxviii. 1. "taken from among men," do we
Heb. v. 1. see the kinship of Christ; but in
Ps. lxxxix. 19. the divinely chosen King the same
wonderful link is given — "One
Deut. xvii. 15. from among thy brethren shalt thou
set king over thee: thou mayest not set a
stranger over thee, which is not thy brother."

How very close this brings us to our glorious Lord! And yet, when we have exhausted all that is contained in the very full and dear idea of "brother," we are led beyond, to realize One
Prov. xviii. 24. who "sticketh *closer* than a brother,"
because no earthly relationship can

entirely shadow forth what Jesus is. And whatever relationship we most value or most miss, will be the very one which, whether by possession or loss, will show us most of Him, and yet fall short of His "reality." For we always have to go beyond the type to reach the antitype.

The King is so "near of kin," that we may come to Him as the tribes of Israel did, and say, "Behold, we are Thy bone and Thy flesh;" finding many a sweet endorsement of the type in His Word. So near of kin, that He is "in all things" "made like unto His brethren;" and whatever is included in the flesh and blood of which we are partakers, sin only excepted, "He also Himself likewise took part of the same."

2 Sam. v. 1.

Eph. v. 30.

Heb. ii. 17.

Ib. ii. 14.

So "near of kin to us," and yet God! Therefore every good thing that we find in near human relationships, we shall find in Jesus in the immeasurable proportion of the divine to the human. Is not this worth thinking out, each for ourselves?—worth seeking to enter into?

But will He acknowledge the kinship? He
Matt. xii. 50. hath said, "Whosoever shall do the will of my Father which is in heaven, the same is my brother and sister and mother." "How beautiful to be Christ's little sister!" said a young disciple. For of course He really means it. Will not this make our prayer
Ps. cxliii. 10. more fervent, "Teach me to do Thy will?"

If the King is indeed near of kin to us, the royal likeness will be recognizable. Can it be
Judg. viii. 18. said of us, "As thou art, so were they; each one resembled the children of a king?" Nor let us shrink from aim-
Ps. xlv. 13. ing at the still higher standard, "The King's daughter is all glorious *within.*"

We must not dwell only on a one-sided kin-
Heb. ii. 11. ship. If "He is not ashamed to call" us "brethren," shall we ever be ashamed to call Him Master? If He is ready to give us all that is implied or involved in near kinship, should we fail to reciprocate with all the love and sympathy and faithfulness which the tie demands on our side?

Also, if we do realize this great privilege, let us prove our loyal love to our Brother-King by "looking for and hasting unto the coming of the day" of His return. Let us not incur the touching reproach, "Ye are my brethren, ye are my bones and my flesh: wherefore then are ye the last to bring back the King?"

2 Pet. iii. 18.

2 Sam. xix. 12.

Joined to Christ in mystic union,
  We Thy members, Thou our Head,
Sealed by deep and true communion,
  Risen with Thee, who once were dead—
Saviour, we would humbly claim
All the power of this Thy name.

Instant sympathy to brighten
  All their weakness and their woe,
Guiding grace their way to lighten,
  Shall Thy loving members know.
All their sorrows Thou dost bear,
All Thy gladness they shall share.

Everlasting life Thou givest,
  Everlasting love to see;
They shall live because Thou livest,
  And their life is hid with Thee.
Safe Thy members shall be found,
When their glorious Head is crowned!

THIRTEENTH DAY.

The Desire of the King.

Ps. xlv. 11. "So shall the King greatly desire thy beauty."

CAN this be for us? What beauty have we that the King can desire? For the more
Isa. vi. 5. we have seen of His beauty, the more we have seen of our own utter ugliness. What, then, can He see? "My
Ezek. xvi. 14. comeliness which I had put upon
Ps. xc. 17. thee." "The beauty of the Lord our God upon us." For "He will
Ps. cxlix. 4. beautify the meek with salvation." And so the desire of the King is set upon us.

Perhaps we have had the dreary idea, "Nobody wants me!" We never need grope in that gloom again, when the King Himself desires us! This desire is love active, love in glow, love going forth, love delighting and longing. It is the strongest representation of the love of Jesus—something far beyond the love of pity or compassion; it is taking pleasure in His people; delighting in them; willing (*i.e.*, putting forth the grand force of His will) that they should be with Him where He is, with Him now, with Him always. It is the love that does not and will not endure separation—the love that can not do without its object. "*So* shall the King desire thy beauty."

Ps. cxlix. 4.
Isa. lxii. 4.
John xvii. 24
Ib. xii. 26.

He gave us a glimpse of this gracious fervor when He said, "With desire I have desired to eat this passover with you before I suffer." With Gethsemane and Calvary in fullest view, His heart's desire was to spend those few last hours in closest intercourse with His disciples. "*So*" did He desire them.

Luke xxii. 15.

Now, if we take the King at His word, and really believe that He thus desires us, can we possibly remain cold-hearted and indifferent to Him? Can we bear the idea of disappointing His love—*such* love—and meeting it with any such pale, cool response as would wound any human heart, "I do not know whether I love you or not!"

Oh, do let us leave off morbidly looking to see exactly how much we love (which is just like trying to warm ourselves with a thermometer, and perhaps only ends in doubting whether we love at all), and look straight away at His love and His desire! Think of Jesus actually wanting you, really desiring your love, not satisfied with all the love of all the angels and saints unless you love Him too—needing that little drop to fill His cup of joy! Is there no answering throb, no responsive glow?

Heb. xii. 2.

> "Lord, let the glow of Thy great love
> Through my whole being shine!"

Perhaps it is upon the emphatic "*so*," as pointing to the context, that the intensity of the emphatic "*greatly*" hinges. It is when the bride forgets her own people and her father's house—that is, when her life and love are altogether given to her Royal Bridegroom—that He "shall *greatly*

Ps. xlv. 10.

desire" her beauty. When His glorious beauty has so filled our eyes, and His incomprehensible
love has so filled our hearts, that He Eph. iii. 19.
is first and most and dearest of all—
when we can say not merely, "The Isa. xxvi. 8.
desire of our souls is to Thy name,"
but "There is *none* upon earth that Ps. lxxiii. 25.
I desire beside Thee"—when thus
we are, to the very depth of our being, really and entirely our Beloved's, then we may add,
in solemn, wondering gladness, Cant. vii. 10.
"And His desire is toward me."

O love surpassing thought,
So bright, so grand, so clear, so true, so glorious;
Love infinite, love tender, love unsought,
Love changeless, love rejoicing, love victorious!
And this great love for us in boundless store;
Christ's everlasting love! What wouldst thou more?

FOURTEENTH DAY.

The Sceptre of the King.

Esth. viii. 4.

"The king held out the golden sceptre."

Amos i. 5.

JESUS is He "that holdeth the sceptre"—the symbol first of kingly right and authority, and next of righteousness and justice. "A sceptre of

Heb. i. 8.

righteousness is the sceptre of Thy kingdom"—"a right sceptre." And

Ps. xlv. 6.

yet the golden sceptre was held out as the sign of sovereign mercy to one who, by "one law of his to put him to death,"

Esth. iv. 11.

must otherwise have perished, "that he may live." Thus, by the combination of direct statement and type, we are shown in this figure the beautiful, perfect meeting of the

"mercy and truth" of our King, Ps. lxxxv. 10.
the "righteousness and peace" of Ib. lxxii. 2, 3.
His kingdom.

Again and again the Holy Ghost repeats this grand blending of seemingly antagonistic attributes, confirming to us in many ways this strong consolation. Heb. vi. 18.

How precious the tiny word *and* becomes as we read, "He is just, *and* having salvation." Zech. ix. 9. "A merciful *and* faithful High-Priest." Heb. ii. 17. "A just God *and* a Saviour." Isa. xlv. 21. We do not half value God's *little* words.

To "the King's enemies," the sceptre is a "rod of iron" (for the word is the same in Hebrew). Ps. xlv. 5. Ib. ii. 9. They can not rejoice in the justice which they defy. To the King's willing subjects it is indeed golden—a beautiful thing and a most precious thing. Ib. ci. 1. We admire and glory in His absolute justice and righteousness; it satisfies the depths of our moral being—it is so strong, so perfect. Rev xv. 3, 4. Isa. xi. 5. Ps. cxix. 164.

His justice is, if we may reverently say so, the strong point of His atoning work. The

costly means of our redemption were paid for
1 Chron. xxi. 24. "at the full price." He fulfilled the
Matt. v. 17. law. There was nothing wanting in
all the work which His Father gave
John xvii. 4. Him to do. He finished it. And
Isa. xlii. 21. His Father was satisfied. Thus He
was just toward His Father, that
1 John i. 9. He might be faithful and just to
forgive us our sins. It is no weak compassion, merely wrought on by misery, but strong, grand, infinite, and equal justice and mercy, balanced, as they never are in human minds. For only
Ezek. xviii. 25. the ways of the Lord are thus
"equal."

Ps. cix. 20, P. B. V. And oh, how "sweet is Thy mer-
Isa. lv. 3. cy!" and just because of the jus-
Esth. iv. 16. tice, how "sure!" Esther said, "If
Ps. cxxxvi. 1. I perish, I perish." So need not we,
"for His mercy endureth forever."
And so, every time we come into the audience-
Cant. i. 4. chamber of our King, we know that
Esth. v. 2. the golden sceptre will be held out to
iv. 11, viii. 3, 4. us, first, "that we may live," and
then for favor after favor. "Let us
Heb. iv. 16. therefore come boldly unto the

throne of grace, that we may obtain mercy, and find grace to help in time of need"—not stand afar off and think about it, and keep our King waiting; but, like Esther, "let us **Heb. x. 22.**
draw near" and "touch the top of **Esth. v. 2.**
the sceptre."

FIFTEENTH DAY.

Cleaving to the King.

2 Sam. xx. 2. "The men of Judah clave unto their king."

FOR it is not a matter of course that coming is followed by cleaving. Even when the King Himself, in His veiled royalty, walked and talked with His few faithful followers,

John vi. 66. "many of His disciples went back, and walked no more with Him.' There was no word of indignation or reproach, only the appeal of infinite pathos from His

Ib. vi. 67. gracious lips, "Will ye also go away?"

Let this sound in our ears to-day, not only in moments of temptation to swerve from truest-hearted loyalty and service, but all through the business of the day; stirring our too easy-going resting into active cleaving;

quickening our following afar off into Matt. xxvi. 58.
following hard after Him; rousing Ps. lxiii. 8.
us to add to the blessed assurance, 1 Chron. xii. 18.
"Thine are we, David!" the bolder
and nobler position, "and *on Thy side!*"

For this cleaving is not a mere terrified clinging for safety—it is the bright, brave resolution, strengthened, not weakened, by the sight of waverers or renegades, to be on 2 Sam. xv. 21
His side, come what may, because He *is* our King, because we love Him, because His cause and His kingdom are so very dear to us.

We can not thus cleave without loosening from other interests. But what matter! Let us be noble for Jesus, like the men of might
who "separated themselves unto 1 Chron. xii. 8.
David," and who "held strongly 1 Chron. xi. 10, marg.
with him in his kingdom." Shall we be mean enough to aim at less, when it is *our Lord Jesus* who would have us Cant. iv. 8.
entirely "with Him?"

It is, after all, the easiest and safest course. The especial friends and "the 1 Kings i. 8.
mighty men which belonged to David," not only did not follow the usurping

Adonijah, but they were never tempted to do
1 Kings i. 26. so. "But me, even me thy servant,
. . . . hath he not called." There
is many a temptation, very powerful and dangerous to a camp-follower, which the enemy
knows it is simply useless to present to one of
Matt. vi. 13. the body-guard. Our Father leads
1 Sam. xxii. 23. us "*not* into temptation," when He
leads us closer to Jesus.

The Bible never speaks of "good resolu-
2 Tim. iii. 10. tions," but again and again of "purpose." And this is what we want,
that "with purpose of heart" we should
Acts xi. 23. "cleave unto the Lord." Have we
this distinct purpose to-day? Do
Josh. xxii. 5, xxiii. 8. we really *mean*, God helping us, to
cleave to our King to-day? Do not
let us dare to go forth to the certain conflicts and temptations of the day with this negative but real disloyalty of want of *purpose* in the
1 John iii. 20. matter. And "if our heart con-
demn us," let us at once turn to
Jer. xiii. 11. Him who says, "I have *caused to*
cleave unto me the whole house of
Israel." His grace shall enable us to cleave unto our King.

SIXTEENTH DAY.

The Joy of the King.

"David the king also rejoiced with great joy." 1 Chron. xxix. 9.

DO not let us think of the joy of our King over His people as only future. While we can not look forward too much to the day when He shall present us "faultless before the presence of His glory (Jude 24.) with exceeding joy," let us not overlook the present gladness which we, even we, who have so often grieved Him, may give to our King.

Elsewhere we hear of the joy of angels over repenting sinners; here we have a glimpse of the joy of the King of (Luke xv. 10.) angels over His consecrated ones. Look at the whole passage—it is full of typical light—and let us take it "for our learning." (Rom. xv. 4.)

1 Chron. xxix. 5. "Who, then, is willing to consecrate his service this day unto the Lord?" Silence is negative here: there must be a definite heart-response if we *are* willing. Are you? If so, when? The King's question says nothing of some day, but of "this day." And the question *is* put to you: if never before, it is sounding in your ears now. Shall
Josh. xxiv. 15. your service be His, "this day," and henceforth? or *not?*

The result of willing consecration of ourselves and our service is always joy. "The
1 Chron. xxix. 9. people rejoiced, for that they offered willingly;" but was it not far more, far sweeter, that their king "also rejoiced with great joy?" How they must have
Ib. xxix. 17. felt when he said, "Now have I seen with joy Thy people which are present here, to offer willingly unto Thee!"

For when a heart and life are willingly offered and fully surrendered to Him, He sees
Isa. liii. 11. of "the travail of His soul" in it; it is a new accomplishment of the work which He came to do: and what then? He
Rom. vi. 13. "is satisfied." If motive were wanting to yield ourselves unto Him,

would it not be more than supplied by the thought that it will be satisfaction and joy to Him "who loved us and washed us from our sins in His own blood?" Rev. i. 5. It seems just the one blessed opportunity given to us of being His true cup-bearers, of bringing the wine of joy to our King; and in so doing He will make our own cups to run over. 1 Kings x. 5. Ps. xxiii. 5.

As our own hearts are filled with the intense joy of consecration to our Lord, a yet intenser glow will come as we remember that His joy is greater than ours, for He is anointed "with the oil of gladness above" His "fellows." Ps. xlv. 7.

Shall not "this day" be "the day of the gladness of His heart?" Will you not consecrate your service to-day unto Him? For then "He will save, He will rejoice over *thee* with joy; He will rest in His love; He will joy over *thee* with singing." Cant. iii. 11. 1 Chron. xxix. 5. Zeph. iii. 17.

Take myself, and I will be,
Ever, *only*, ALL for Thee!

SEVENTEENTH DAY.

Rest on the Word of the King.

2 Sam. xiv. 17. "The word of my lord the king shall now be for rest" (*margin*).

HERE is the whole secret of rest from the very beginning to the very end. The *word* of our King is all we have and all we need for deep, utter heart-rest, which no surface
Job xxxiv. 29. waves of this troublesome world can
Isa. xiv. 3. disturb. What gave "rest from thy sorrow and from thy fear" at the very first, when we wanted salvation and peace? It was not some vague, pleasing impression, some undefinable hush that came to us (or if it was,
Eccl. viii. 4. the unreality of the rest was soon
1 Tim. i. 15. proved), but some word of our King
2 Thess. ii. 13. which we saw to be worthy of all acceptation; we believed it, and by
Heb. iv. 2, 3. it Jesus gave us rest.

There is no other means of rest for all the

way but the very same. The moment we simply believe any word of the King, we find that it is truly "for rest" about the point to which it refers. And if we would but *go on taking* the King's word about every single thing, we should *always* find it, then and there, "for rest." Every flutter of unrest may, if we look honestly into it, be traced to not entirely and absolutely taking the King's word. His words are *enough* for rest at all times, and in all circumstances; therefore we are sinning the great sin of unbelief whenever we allow ourselves in any phase of unrest. It is not infirmity, but sin, to neglect to make use of the promises which He meant for our strong consolation and continual help. And we ought not to acquiesce in the shadows which are only around us, because we do not hear, or hearing do not heed, God's call into the sunshine.

Mark ix. 23.

Heb. vi. 18.

Take the slightest and commonest instances. If we have an entire and present belief in "My grace is sufficient for thee," or, "Lo, I am with you alway," should we feel nervous at anything He calls us

2 Cor. xii. 9.
Matt. xxviii. 20.

to do for Him? Would not that word be
indeed "for rest" in the moment of need--
Phil. iv. 19. "rest from the hard bondage" of
Isa. xiv. 3. service to which we feel unequal?
Heb. iv. 16. Have we not sometimes found it so,
and if so, why not always? I see nothing
about "sometimes" in any of His promises. If
we have an entire and present belief that "all
Rom. viii. 28. things work together for good," or
Ps. cvii. 7. that He leads us "forth by the right
way," should we feel worried when some one
thing seems to work wrong, and some one yard
of the way is not what we think straightest?

1 John ii. 25. We lean upon the word of the
King for everlasting life, why not
for daily life also? For it shall "*now* be for
rest;" only try it to-day, "now," and see if it
shall not be so! When He says "perfect
Isa. xxvi. 3. peace," He can not mean imperfect
2 Chron. xxxii. 8. peace. "The people rested themselves upon the words of Hezekiah,
king of Judah." Just so simply let us rest upon the words of our King, Jesus!

EIGHTEENTH DAY.

The Business of the King.

"The king's business required haste." 1 Sam. xxi. 8.

AND yet there is no other business about which average Christians take it so easy. They "must" go their usual round, they "must" write their letters, they "must" pay off their visits and other social claims, they "must" do all that is expected of them; and then, after this and that and the other thing is cleared off, they will do what they can of the King's business. They do not say "must" about that, unless it is some part of His business which is undertaken at second-hand, and with more sense of responsibility to one's clergyman than to one's King. Is this being faithful and loyal and single-hearted? If it has been so, oh, let it be so no more! How

Luke xiv. 20.

Ib. ix. 59, 61.

Eph. vi. 5, 6.

Matt. xvii. 8. can "Jesus *Only*" be our motto,
Ib. vi. 33. when we have not even said "Jesus *first?*"

The King's business *requires* haste. It is always pressing, and may never be put off. Much of it has to do with souls which may be
Luke xii. 20. in eternity to-morrow; and with opportunities which are gone forever if not used then and there; there is no "con-
Acts xxiv. 25. venient season" for it but "to-day."
Heb. iii. 13. Often it is not really done at all, because it is not done in the spirit of holy haste. We meet an unconverted friend again and again, and beat about the bush, and think to gain quiet influence and make way gradually, and call it judicious not to be in a hurry, when the real reason is that we are wanting in holy eagerness and courage to do the King's true business with that soul, and in nine such cases out of ten nothing ever comes out of it; but
1 Kings xx. 40. "As thy servant was busy here and there, he was gone." Have we not found it so?

Delay in the Lord's errands is next to disobedience, and generally springs out of it, or

issues in it. "God commanded me 2 Chron.
to make haste." Let us see to it xxxv. 21.
that we can say, "I made haste, and Ps. cxix. 60.
delayed not to keep Thy commandments."

We never know what regret and punishment delay in the King's business may bring upon ourselves. Amasa "tarried longer
than the set time which he (the king) 2 Sam. xx. 5.
had appointed him," and the result was death to himself. Contrast the result in Abigail's
case, where, except she had hasted, 1 Sam. xxv.
her household would have perished. 34.

We find four rules for doing the King's business in His word. We are to do it—first,
"Heartily;" second, "Diligently;" Col. iii. 23.
third, "Faithfully;" fourth, "*Speed-* Ezra vii. 23.
ily." Let us ask Him to give us 2 Chron. xxxiv. 12.
the grace of energy to apply them Ezra vii. 21.
this day to whatever He indicates as our part of His business, remembering that *He* said
"I *must* be about my Father's Luke ii. 49.
business." John ix. 4.

Especially in that part of it which is between Himself and ourselves alone, let us never delay. Oh, the incalculable blessings that we have

already lost by putting off our own dealings
1 Sam. xxv. 18. with our King! Abigail first "made
haste" to meet David for mere
safety; soon afterward, she again "hasted and
Ib. xxv. 42. arose and went after the messengers
of David, and became his wife."

Thus hasting, we shall rise from privilege to
Ps. lxxxiv. 7. privilege, and "go from strength to
strength."

What shall be our word for Jesus? Master, give it day by day;
Ever as the need arises, teach Thy children what to say.
Give us holy love and patience; grant us deep humility,
That of self we may be emptied, and our hearts be full of Thee;
Give us zeal and faith and fervor, make us winning, make us wise,
Single-hearted, strong and fearless;—Thou hast called us, we will rise!
Let the might of Thy good Spirit go with every loving word;
And by hearts prepared and opened, be our message always heard!

NINETEENTH DAY.

The Readiness of the King's Servants.

"Thy servants are ready to do whatso- 2 Sam. xv. 15
ever my lord the king shall appoint."

THIS is the secret of steady and unruffled gladness in "the business of 1 Chron. xxvi. 30.
the Lord, and the service of the King," whether we are "over the Ib. xxvi. 20.
treasures of the house of God," or "for the outward business over Ib. xxvi. 29.
Israel."

It makes all the difference! If we are really and always, and equally ready to do John ii. 5.
whatsoever the King appoints, all the trials and vexations arising from any change in His appointments, great or small, simply do not exist. If He appoints me to work there, shall

Josh. i. 16. I lament that I am not to work here? If He appoints me to wait in-doors to-day, am I to be annoyed because I am not to work out-of-doors? If I meant to *write* His messages this morning, shall I grumble because He sends interrupting visitors, rich or poor, to
Sam. ix. 3. whom I am to *speak* them, or "show kindness" for His sake, or at least
1 Pet. iii. 8. obey His command, "Be courte-
Rom. vi. 13. ous?" If all my "members" are really at His disposal, why should I be put out if to-day's appointment is some simple work for my hands or errands for my feet, instead of some seemingly more important doing of head or tongue?

Does it seem a merely ideal life? Try it! begin at once; before you venture away from this quiet moment, ask your King to take you "wholly" into His service, and place all the hours of this day quite simply at His disposal, and ask Him to make and keep you *ready* to
Jas. iv. 14. do just exactly what He appoints. Never mind about to-morrow; one day at a time is enough. Try it to-day, and see if it is not a day of strange, almost *curious*

peace, so sweet that you will be only too thankful, when to-morrow comes, to ask Him to take it also—till it will become a blessed habit to hold yourself simply and "wholly at Thy commandment" "for *any* manner of service." 1 Chron. xxviii. 21.

Then will come, too, an indescribable and unexpected sense of freedom, and a total relief from the self-imposed bondage of "having to get through" what we think lies before us. For "of the children of Israel did Solomon make no bondmen." 1 Kings ix. 22.

Then, too, by thus being ready, moment by moment, for whatsoever He shall appoint, we realize very much more that we are not left alone, but that we are dwelling "with the King for His work." 1 Chron. iv. 23. Thus the very fact of an otherwise vexatious interruption is transmuted into a Ps. cxxxix. 5. precious proof of the nearness of the King. His interference implies His interest and His presence.

The "whatsoever" is not necessarily active work. It may be waiting (whether half an hour or half a life-time), learning, suffering, sit ting still. But, dear fellow-servants of ' my Lord the King," shall we be less ready for these, if any of them are His appointments for to-day? "Whatsoever the king did pleased all the people."

2 Sam. iii. 36.

"Ready" implies something of preparation—not being taken by surprise. So let us ask Him to prepare us for all that He is preparing for us. And may "the hand of God give" us "one heart to do the commandment of the King!"

2 Chron. xxx. 12.

"Lord, I have given my life to Thee,
And every day and hour is Thine;
What Thou appointest let them be;
Thy will is better, Lord, than mine."
—A. L. WARING.

TWENTIETH DAY.

The Friendship of the King.

"He that loveth pureness of heart, for the grace of his lips the king shall be his friend." Prov. xxii. 11.

"WHO can say, I have made my heart clean, I am pure?" Who must not despair of the friendship of the King if this were the condition? But His wonderful condescension in promising His friendship bends yet lower in its tenderly-devised condition. Not to the absolutely pure in heart, but to the perhaps very sorrowfully longing lover of that pureness come the gracious words, "The King shall be his Friend." Ib. xx. 9. Hab. i. 13. Matt. v. 8.

Yet there must be some proof of this love; and it is found in "the grace of his lips." "For out of the abundance of the heart, the mouth speaketh." Here, Matt. xii. 44.

again, we stop and question our claim; for our
Col. iv. 6. speech has not always been "with
Matt. xii. 36. grace;" and the memory of many a
graceless and idle word rises to bar
it. How, then, shall the King be our Friend?
Ps. xlv. 2. Another word comes to our help:
"Grace is poured into *thy* lips"—
Luke iv. 22. grace that overflowed in gracious
John vii. 46. words, such as never man spake,
perfectly holy and beautiful; and
we look up to our King and plead that He has
Himself fulfilled the condition in which we
have failed—that this is part of the righteousness which He wrought for us, and which is
Rom. iii. 22. really unto us and upon us, because
we believe in Him; and so, for the
grace of His own lips, the King shall be our
Friend.

Who has not longed for an ideal and yet a
Ps. cxxxix. 2. real friend—one who should exactly
Mark vi. 30. understand us, to whom we could
tell everything, and in whom we
could altogether confide—one who should be
Rev. xix. 11. very wise and very true—one of
John xiii. 1. whose love and unfailing interest we

could be certain? There are other points for which we could not hope—that this friend should be very far above us, and yet the very
nearest and dearest, always with us, Matt. xxviii. 20.
always thinking of us, always doing
kind and wonderful things for us; Ps. xl. 17.
undertaking and managing every- Ib. lvii. 2.
thing; forgetting nothing, failing in Isa. xxxviii. 14.
nothing; quite certain never to Zeph. iii. 5. Mal. iii. 6.
change and never to die—so that Heb. vii. 24.
this one grand friendship should fill
our lives, and that we really never 1 Pet. v. 7.
need trouble about anything for
ourselves any more at all.

Such is our Royal Friend, and more; for no human possibilities of friendship can illustrate
what He is to those to whom He John xv. 14.
says, "Ye are my friends." We,
even we, may look up to our glorious King, our Lord and our God, Ib. xx. 28.
and say, "This is my Beloved, and Cant. v. 16.
this is my Friend!" And then we, even we,
may claim the privilege of being 1 Chron.
"the King's companion" and the xxvii. 33.
"King's friend." 1 Kings iv. 5.

TWENTY-FIRST DAY

The Light of the King's Countenance.

Prov. xvi. 15. "In the light of the king's countenance is life."

BUT first fell the solemn words, "Thou hast set our secret sins in the light of Thy
Ps. xc. 8. countenance." That was the first we knew of its brightness; and to some its revelation has been so terrible, that they can even understand how the Lord "shall
2 Thess. ii. 8. destroy" the wicked "with the brightness of His coming." Yet,
Rev. i. 14. though we feel that "His eyes were
Prov. xx. 8. as a flame of fire," we found also that our "King that sitteth in the throne of judgment, scattereth away all evil with His eyes;" and that it was when we stood

in that light, that we found the power of the precious blood of Jesus, the Anointed One, to cleanse us from all sin. 1 John i. 7.

This gives new value to the promise, "They *shall* walk, O Lord, in the light of Thy countenance;" for it is when we walk in the light that we may claim and do realize the fullness of its power and preciousness—not for fitful and occasional cleansing, but for a glorious, perpetual, present cleansing from all sin. Do not let us translate it into another tense for ourselves, and read, "*did* cleanse last time we knelt and asked for it," but keep to the tense which the Holy Ghost has written, and meet the foe-flung darts of doubt with faith's great answer, "The blood of Jesus Christ His Son cleanseth (i. e., *goes on cleansing*) us from all sin." Ps. lxxxix. 15. Rev. xxii. 18, 19. Eph. vi. 16.

Thus the light of His countenance shall save us. Look at Ps. xliv. 3, where we see it as the means of past salvation, and then at Ps. xliii. 5, where the Psalmist anticipates praise for its future help; while the two are Ps. xliv. 3. Ib. xliii. 5.

beautifully linked by the marginal reading of the latter, which makes it present salvation: "Thy presence *is* salvation."

Then follows peace. The waves are stilled, and the storm-clouds flee away noiselessly and
Num. vi. 26. swiftly and surely, when He lifts up
the light of His countenance upon
2 Sam. xxiii. 4. us, and gives us peace. For this
uplifting is the shining forth of His favor—the smile instead of the frown; and as we walk in the light of it, the peace will grow into joy, and we shall be even here and now
Ps. xxi. 6. "exceeding glad with Thy countenance," while every step will bring us nearer to the resurrection joy of Christ
Acts ii. 28. Himself, saying with Him, "Thou
shalt make me full of joy with Thy countenance."

So we shall find day by day, that in the light of the King's countenance is cleansing, salvation, peace, joy—and do not these make up life, the new life, the glad life of the children of the King!

Ps. iv. 6. "Lord, lift Thou up the light of
Thy countenance upon us" this

day, and in it let us have life, yea, John x. 10.
"life more abundantly."

"He that followeth me shall not Ib. viii. 12.
walk in darkness, but shall have the light of life."

TWENTY-SECOND DAY.

The Tenderness of the King.

2 Sam. xviii. "And the king commanded, saying,
5. Deal gently for my sake with the young
man, even with Absalom."

EVEN with Absalom! Even with the heartless, deliberate traitor and rebel.
Ib. xv. 2–11. We must recollect clearly what he was, to appreciate the exquisite tenderness of David in such a command to his rough war-captains in such untender times. For the sake of his people and his kingdom, he must send them forth against him, but the deep love gushes out in the bidding, "Deal gently for my sake."

It was no new impulse. When Amnon was
2 Sam. xiii. murdered, the king "wept very
36, 37. sore," and "mourned for his son
every day;" and yet, when the fratricide had

fled, "the soul of King David longed to go forth unto him," and "the king's heart was toward Absalom." And when God's own vengeance fell upon the wicked son, David's lamentation over him is perhaps unparalleled in its intensity of pathos among the records of human tenderness.

2 Sam. xiii. 39.
2 Sam. xiv. 1.
Ib. xviii. 33.

Turn to the Antitype, and see the divine tenderness of our King. Again and again it gleams out, whether He Himself wept, or whether He said, "Weep not"—whether in the tender look, the tender word, or the tender touch of gentlest mercy. The Gospels are full of His tenderness. There is not room here even for the bare mention of the instances of it; but will you not give a little time to searching quietly for them, so that, reading them under the teaching of the Holy Spirit, you may get a concentrated view of the wonderful tenderness of Jesus, and yield your heart to be moved by it, and your spirit to be so penetrated by it, that you may share it and reflect it. Remember

Luke xix. 43.
Ib. vii. 13.
Ib. xxii. 61.
John xiv. 1.
Matt. viii. 15.
John xiv. 26.

that in such a search we learn not only what He did and said, nor only what He was, but what He *is;* and in all His recorded tenderness we are looking into the *present* heart of Jesus, and seeing what we shall find for our-
Acts i. 11. selves as we have need. For He is
"this same Jesus" to-day.

Then let us glance at the volume of our own experience. Who that has had any dealings with Christ at all, but must bear witness that He has indeed dealt gently with us. Has not even suffering been sweet when it showed us
Lam. iii. 32. more of this? What if He had ever
Ps. ciii. 10. "dealt with us after our sins!"
Job xi. 6. But He never did, and never will.
He hath dealt gently, and will deal gently with us, for His own sake, and according to His
Jer. xxxi. 3. own heart, from the first drawings
of His loving-kindness, on throughout the measureless developments of His everlasting love. Not till we are in heaven shall
Ps. xviii. 35. we know the full meaning of "Thy
gentleness hath made me great."

May we not recognize a command in this, as well as a responsibility to follow the example

of the "gentleness of Christ?" 2 Cor. x. 1.
Perhaps next time we are tempted to be a little harsh or hasty with an erring or offending one, the whisper will come, "Deal gently, for my sake!"

Return!
O erring, yet beloved!
I wait to bind thy bleeding feet, for keen
And rankling are the thorns where thou hast been;
I wait to give thee pardon, love, and rest.
(Is not my joy to see thee safe and blest?)
Return! I wait to hear once more thy voice,
To welcome thee anew, and bid thy heart rejoice!

Return!
O chosen of my love!
Fear not to meet thy beckoning Saviour's view;
Long ere I called thee by thy name, I knew
That very treacherously thou wouldst deal;
Now I have seen thy ways—yet I will heal.
Return! Wilt thou yet linger far from Me?
My wrath is turned away, I have redeemèd thee!

TWENTY-THIRD DAY.

The Token of the King's Grace.

2 Sam. xiv. 22. "To-day thy servant knoweth that I have found grace in thy sight, my Lord, O king, in that the king hath fulfilled the request of his servant."

AN answered prayer makes us glad for its own sake. But there is grace behind the gift which is better and more gladdening than the gift itself. For which is most valued, the "engaged ring," or the favor of which it is the token? Setting aside judicial answers to un-
Ps. cvi. 15. spiritual prayers, which an honest
Hos. xiii. 11, etc. conscience will have no difficulty
in distinguishing, the servants of the King may take it that His answers to their re-
John iii. 22. quests are proofs and tokens of His
grace and favor—of His real, and

present, and personal love to themselves individually.

When they are receiving few or none, they should search for the cause, lest it should be some hidden or unrecognized sin. For "if I regard iniquity in my heart, the Lord will not hear me;" so *never* let us go on comfortably and easily when He is silent to us. And instead of envying others who get "such wonderful answers," "let us search and try our ways."

Job x. 2.
1 Sam. xxviii. 6.
Ps. xix. 12.
Ib. lxvi. 18.
Lam. iii. 40.

Personal acceptance comes first. We must be "accepted in the Beloved" before we can look to be answered through the Beloved. Is there a doubt about this, and a sigh over the words? There need not be; for now, at this moment, the old promise stands with its unchangeable welcome to the weary: "Him that cometh to me I will in no wise cast out." Then, if you come, now, at this moment, on the strength of His word, you *can not* be rejected; and if not rejected, there is nothing but one blessed alternative—"accepted!"

Eph. i. 6.
John vi. 37.
Heb. vii. 25.

Then come the answers! As surely as the
prayers go up from the accepted one, so surely
will the blessings come down. When Esther
Esth. v. 3. had touched the golden sceptre,
"*then* said the king unto her, What
wilt thou, Queen Esther, and what is thy request? it shall be even given thee to the half
of the kingdom." But there is no "half" in
Matt. xxi. 22. our King's promise. He says, "All
John xiv. 13. things" and "whatsoever." And
He *does* "do exceeding abundantly above all
Eph. iii. 20. that we ask or think," and more than
1 Kings x. 13. fulfills our little scanty requests.

And *then*, by every fresh fulfillment we should receive ever new assurance of our acceptance—*then* (shall it not be "to-day?") as we give thanks for each gracious answer, we may look up confidingly and joyfully, and say, "Thy servant *knoweth* that I have found grace
2 Sam. xxv. in thy sight." For He says, "See,
35. I have hearkened to thy voice, and
have accepted thy person."

Eph. i. 6. Accepted, Perfect, and Complete,
Col. i. 28. For God's inheritance made meet!
Col. ii. 10. How true, how glorious, and how sweet!

TWENTY-FOURTH DAY.

The Omniscience of the King.

"There is no matter hid from the king." 2 Sam. xviii. 13.

THE very attributes which are full of terror to "the King's enemies," are full of comfort to the King's friends. Ps. xlv. 5. Thus His omniscience is like the pillar, which was "a cloud and darkness" to the Egyptians, but "gave light by night" to the Israelites. Ex. xiv. 20.

The king's own General complained of a man who did not act precisely as he himself would have acted. 2 Sam. xviii. 11. In his reply he uses these words, "There is no matter hid from the king." The appeal was final, and Joab had no more to say. When others say, like Joab, "'*Why* didst thou not do so and so?" and we know or find that full reasons can not be given or can not be understood, what rest it is to fall back upon the certainty that our King knows all about it! When we are wearied out with trying to make people understand, how restful it is that no explanations are wanted when we come to speak to Him! "All things are naked and opened unto the eyes of Him with whom we have to do;" and the more we have to do with Him, the more glad and thankful we shall be that there is "not anything" hid from the King.

Job xxiii. 10. Heb. iv. 13. 1 Kings x. 3.

In perplexities—when we can not understand what is going on around us—can not tell whither events are tending—can not tell what to do, because we can not see into or through the matter before us—let us be calmed and steadied and made patient by the thought that what is hidden from us is not hidden from Him. If He chooses to guide us blindfold, let Him do it! It will not make the least difference to the reality and rightness of the guidance.

Isa. xlii. 16. Ps. cvii. 7.

In mysteries—when we see no clue—when
we can not at all understand God's Rom. ix. 33,
partial revelation—when we can not 34.
lift the veil that hangs before His secret coun-
sel—when we can not pierce the holy
darkness that enshrouds His ways, Ps. xcvii. 2.
or tread the great deep of His judg- Ib. xxxvi. 6.
ments where His footsteps are not Ib. lxxvii. 19.
known—is it not enough that even these mat-
ters are not hid from our King? "My father
will do nothing, either great or small, 1 Sam. xx. 2.
but he will show it me." "For the John v. 20.
Father loveth the Son, and showeth Him all
things that Himself doeth."

Our King could so easily reveal everything to us, and make everything so clear! It would be nothing to Him to tell us all our questions. 1 Kings x. 3. When He does not, can not we trust Him, and just be satisfied that He knows, and would tell us if it were best? He has "many things to say" unto us, John xvi. 12. but He waits till we can bear them.

May we be glad that even our sins are "not hid" from Him? Yes, surely, for He who

Ps. cxxxix. 1. knows all can and will cleanse all.
Isa. xlviii. 8. He has searched us and known us,
as we should shrink from knowing ourselves,
and *yet* He has pardoned, and *yet* He loves!

TWENTY-FIFTH DAY.

The Power of the King's Word.

"Where the word of a king is, there is power." Eccl. viii. 4.

THEN the question is, *Where* is it? "Let the word of Christ dwell *in you* richly," and "there," even "in you," will be power. Col. iii. 16. Heb. ii. 9.

The Crowned One, who is now "upholding all things by the word of His power," hath said, "I have given them Thy word." And those who have received this great gift, "not as the word of men, but, as it is in truth, the word of God," know that "there is power" with it, because it "effectually worketh also" in them. Ib. i. 3. John xvii. 14. 1 Thess. ii. 13.

They know its life-giving power, for they can say, "Thy word hath quickened me;" and its life-sustaining power, Ps. cxix. 5.

Matt. iv. 4. for they live "by every word that
proceedeth out of the mouth of
Ps. cxix. 11. God." They can say, "Thy word
have I hid in my heart, that I might
not sin against Thee;" for in proportion as
the word of the King is present in the heart,
"*there* is power" against sin. Then let us use
John vi. 63. this means of absolute power more,
Ib. xvii. 17. and more life and more holiness will
be ours.

Luke iv. 32. "His word was with power" in
Capernaum of old, and it will be
with the same power in any place nowadays.
Isa. lv. 11. His word can not fail; it "shall not
return void;" it "*shall* prosper."
1 Sam. iii. 19. Therefore, when our "words fall to
the ground," it only proves that they
were not His words. So what we want is not
merely that His power may accompany our
word, but that we may not speak our own at
all, but simply and only the very "word of the
King." Then there will be power in and with
1 Kings xxii. 34. it. Bows drawn at a venture hit in
a way that astonishes ourselves, when
Ps. xlv. 5. God puts His own arrows on the
string.

There is great comfort and help in taking this literally. Why ask a little when we may ask much? The very next time we want to speak or write "a word for Jesus" Heb. iii. 13.
(and of course that ought to be to-day), let us ask Him to give us not merely a general idea what to say, but to give us literally every single word, and "they shall Prov. xxii. 18.
be withal fitted in thy lips."

For He will not say, "Thou hast 2 Kings ii. 10.
asked a hard thing," though it is far more than asking for the mantle of any prophet. He says, "Behold, I have put My Jer. i. 9.
words in thy mouth." This was not for Jeremiah alone, for soon after we read, "He that hath My word, let him Ib. xxiii. 28.
speak My word faithfully" (for we must not overlook our responsibility in the matter); and then follows the grand declaration of its power, even when spoken by feeble human lips: "Is not My word like Ib. xxiii. 29.
as a fire? saith the Lord; and like a hammer that breaketh the rock in pieces?" "Behold, I will make My words in Ib. v. 14.
thy mouth fire."

2 Cor. iii. 5. If we are not even "sufficient of ourselves to *think* anything as of ourselves," how much less to *speak* anything! Num. xxii. 38. "Have I now any power at all to say anything? The word that God putteth in my mouth, that shall I speak." We 2 Cor. iv. 7. would rather have it so, "that the excellency of the power may be of God, and not of us." Our ascended King has Matt. xxviii. 18, 19. said, "All power is given unto Me. Go ye *therefore*." That is enough Ps. cxix. 42. for me; and "I trust in Thy word.'

Resting on the faithfulness of Christ our Lord,
Resting on the fullness of His own sure word,
Resting on His power, on His love untold,
Resting on His covenant secured of old.

TWENTY-SIXTH DAY.

The Name of the King.

"A King shall reign. And this is His name whereby He shall be called, THE LORD OUR RIGHTEOUSNESS." Jer. xxiii. 5, 6.

WE can not do without this most wonderful name. It can never be an old story to us. It is always a "new name" in freshness and beauty and power. It is our daily need and our daily joy. For strength it is indeed "a strong tower; the righteous runneth into it, and is safe." For sweetness it is "as ointment poured forth." In it we see at once the highest height and the deepest depth, Jehovah, God of God, Light of Light, and our need of a righteousness which is not our own at all, because we have none. We stand as

Rev. iii. 12.

Prov. xviii. 10.

Cant. i. 3.

upon an Alpine slope, face to face with the highest, grandest, purest summit above, and the darkest, deepest valley below, seeing more of the height because of the depth, and more of the depth because of the height.

Heb. i. 4. Jesus our King "hath by inheritance obtained a more excellent name" than angels, for His Father has given
Jer. xxiii. 6, marg. Him His own name—"He shall be called Jehovah." But this alone would be too great, too far off for us; it might find echoes among the harpings of sinless angels, but not among the sighings of sinful souls. And so the name was completed for us, by the very word that expresses our truest, deepest, widest, most perpetual need, and the Holy Ghost revealed the Son of God to us as "Jehovah our Righteousness."

Do not let us be content with theoretically understanding and correctly holding the doctrine of justification by faith. Turn from the words to the reality, from the theory to the Person, and as a little, glad, wondering child, look at the simple, wonderful truth. That "the Righteousness of God' (how magnificent!) is "unto all and upon all them that believe;" therefore, at this very moment, unto and upon you and me, instead of our own filthy rags, so that we stand clothed and beautiful in the very sight of God, *now;* and Jesus can say, "Thou art all fair, my love," *now!* That it is not any finite righteousness, which might not quite cover the whole—might not be quite enough to satisfy God's all-searching eye; not *a* righteousness, but *The* Righteousness of God; and this no abstract attribute, but a Person, real, living, loving—covering us with His own glorious apparel, representing us before His Father, Christ Jesus Himself "made unto us Righteousness!" This to-day and this forever, for "His name shall endure forever."

Rom. iii. 22. Isa. lxiv. 6. Zech. iii. 4. 5. Cant. iv. 7. Phil. iii. 9. Isa. lxiii. 1. 1 Cor. i. 30. Ps. lxxii. 17.

It is in His kingly capacity that this glorious name is given to Him. For only by "*submitting* ourselves to the Righteousness of God," can we have "the blessedness of the man unto whom God imputeth righteous-

Rom. x. 3. Ib. iv. 6.

ness without works." There can be no compromise—it must be His only or ours only. He must be our King, or He will not be our Righteousness.

TWENTY-SEVENTH DAY.

Working with the King.

"There they dwelt with the king for his work." 1 Chron. iv. 23.

"THERE!"—Not in any likely place at all, not in the palace, not in "the city of the great king," but in about the last place one would have expected, "among plants and hedges." It does not even seem clear why they were "there" at all, for they were potters, not gardeners—thus giving us the combination of simple labor of the hands, carried on in out-of-the-way places; and yet they were dwellers with the king, and workers with the king.

Ps. xlviii. 2.
1 Chron. iv. 23.

The lesson seems twofold—First, that anywhere and everywhere we too may dwell "with the King for His work." We may be in a very

unlikely or unfavorable place for this—it may be in a literal country life, with little enough to
Ps. lxviii. 24. be seen of the "goings" of the King around us; it may be among hedges of all sorts, hinderances in all directions; it may be, furthermore, with our hands full of all manner of pottery for our daily task. No matter! The King who placed us "there" will come
Job iii. 23. and dwell there with us; the hedges are all right, or He would soon do away with them, and it does not follow that
Matt. xxi. 33. what seems to hinder our way may not be for its very protection; and as for the pottery, why, that is just exactly what He has seen fit to put into our hands, and
Mark xiii. 34. therefore it is, for the present, "His work."

Secondly, that the dwelling and the working must go together. If we are indeed dwelling with the King, we shall be working for Him
Gal. vi. 10. too, "as we have opportunity." The working will be as the dwelling—a settled, regular thing, whatever form it may
John xv. 5. take at His appointment. Nor will His work ever be done when we are

not dwelling with Him. It will be our own work then, not His, and it will not 1 Cor. iii. 14. "abide." We shall come under the condemnation of the vine which was pronounced "empty," because "he Hos. x. 1. bringeth forth fruit unto himself."

We are to dwell with the King "for His work;" but He will see to it that it shall be for a great deal besides—for a great 2 Sam. vii. 21. continual reward according to His 1 Kings x. 13. own heart and out of His royal bounty—for peace, for power, for love, for gladness, for likeness to Himself.

"Laborers together with God!" 1 Cor. iii. 9. "workers together with Him!" "the 2 Cor. vi. 1. Lord working with" us! admitted Mark xvi. 20. into divine fellowship of work!—will not this thought ennoble everything He gives us to do to-day, even if it is "among plants and hedges!' Even the pottery will be grand!

"Be strong, all ye people of the Hag. ii. 4. land, saith the Lord, and work, FOR I am with you, saith the Lord of hosts."

TWENTY-EIGHTH DAY.

The Recompense of the King.

2 Sam. xix. 36. "Why should the king recompense it me with such a reward?"

BARZILLAI "had provided the king of sustenance while he lay at Mahanaim,"
Ib. xix. 32. exiled from his royal city. When the day of triumphant return came,
Ib. xix. 33. David said to him, "Come thou over with me, and I will feed thee with me in Jerusalem." This was the "reward."

But what a privilege and delight it must have been to the loyal old man! And to come nearer, what a continual joy it must have been
Luke viii. 3. to the women who "ministered" to the exiled King of heaven "of their substance." How *very* much one would have liked a share in that ministry!

Is there *any* loving wish which our King does not meet? Was it not most thoughtful of Him to appoint His continual representatives, so that we might (John xii. 8.) always and every one of us have the opportunity of ministering *to Him!* These opportunities are wider than we sometimes think; some limit His "gracious Inasmuch" (Matt. xxv. 40.) to services for His sake to the poor only. Yet the "strangers" whom (Deut. x. 19.) He bids us love, may be rich in all but the friendliness and kindness which we may show them; and the "sick" may be those among our own dear ones who need our ministry. Why should we fancy it is only those who are *not* near and dear to us, to whom we may minister "as unto Him?" (Eph. vi. 7.)

But oh, what little services are our cups of cold water! and how utterly ashamed (Mark ix. 41.) we feel of ever having thought any of them wearying or irksome, when we look at "the recompense of the reward,"—"*such* a reward!" (Heb. xi. 26.) Is there one of us whose heart has not thrilled at the mere imagining of what it will be to hear "the King

Matt. xxv. 34. say, Come, ye blessed!" Then
what will it be to enter into the full-
2 Sam. xix. 33. ness of the reward, to "come over
with" Him, and dwell with Him al-
Rev. xxi. 10. ways in "the holy Jerusalem," and
Ib. iii. 12. "go no more out."

"*Why* should the king recompense it me with
1 Sam. xxvii. 5. such a reward?" "*Why* should
thy servant dwell in the royal city
with thee?" For there is such a tremendous disproportion between the work and the reward, though such a glorious proportion between His love and His reward.

And yet there is a beautiful fitness in it.
Luke xiv. 15. The banquet of everlasting joy for
Matt. xxv. 35, etc. those who gave Him meat; the river
Ps. xxxvi. 8. of His pleasures for those who gave
John xiv. 2. Him drink; the mansions in the Father's home for those who took the stranger
Rev. vii. 13. in; the white robes for those who
clothed the naked; the tree of life
Ib. xxii. 2. and "no more pain" for those who
Ib. xxi. 4. visited the sick; the "glorious lib-
Rom. viii. 21. erty" for those who came unto the
prisoner; the crown of all, the repeatedly-

promised "with Me," for those who were content to be with His sorrowful or suffering ones for His sake. *Why* all this? I suppose we shall keep on asking that forever!

John xvii. 24.

TWENTY-NINTH DAY.

The Salvation of the King.

Isa. xxx. 22. "The Lord is our King; He will save us."

THE thought of salvation is constantly connected with that of kingship. Type, illustration, and prophecy combine them.
1 Sam. ix. 16. "Thou shalt anoint him . . . . that
2 Sam. iii. 19. he may save my people." "By the
hand of my servant David I will
Ib. xix. 9. save my people." "The king saved
us." "A King shall reign; in His
Jer. xxiii. 5, 6. days, Judah shall be saved." "Thy
Zech. ix. 9. King cometh, ... having salvation."

Because Jesus is our Saviour, He has the right to be our King; but again, because He

is King, He is qualified to be our Saviour; and we never know Him fully as Saviour till we have fully received Him as King. His kingship gives the strength to His priesthood. It
is as the Royal Priest of the order Heb. vii. 1, 17.
of Melchisedec that He is "able to Ib. vii. 25.
save." Thus He is "a Saviour, and Isa. xix. 20.
a Great One," "mighty to save." Ib. lxiii. 1.

Our King has not only 1 Sam. xix. 5.
"wrought," and "brought," and Isa. lxiii. 5.
"made known His salvation," but Ps. xcviii. 2.
He Himself *is* our salvation. The very names seem used interchangeably. Isaiah says, "Say
ye to the daughter of Zion, Behold, Isa. lxii. 11.
thy *Salvation* cometh;" Zechariah Zech. ix. 9.
bids her rejoice, for "Behold, thy *King* cometh." Again, Isaiah says, "Mine
eyes have seen the *King;*" and Isa. vi. 5.
Simeon echoes, "Mine eyes have
seen thy *Salvation,*" as he looks Luke ii. 30.
upon the infant Jesus, the Light to
lighten the Gentiles; reminding us Ib. ii. 32.
again of David's words, "The Lord
is my light and my salvation." Ps. xxvii. 1.

It is because we need salvation, because we

are surrounded by enemies and dangers, and have no power to help ourselves, and have no
Hos. xiii. 10. other help or hope, that He says, "I will be thy King; where is any other that may save thee?" There is no other.
Isa. lix. 16. "He saw that there was no man,"
Hos. xiii. 4. and He says, "There is no Saviour beside me."

What is our response? David begins a
Ps. lxii. 1. psalm by saying, "Truly, my soul waiteth upon God: from Him cometh my salvation;" but he quickly raises the
Ib. lxii. 2. key, and sings, "He *only* is my salvation." Perhaps we have long been quite clear that He *only* is our salvation
2 Thess. i. 9. from "everlasting destruction;" but are we equally clear that He *only* is (not will be, but *is*) our present salvation from everything from which we want to be
Luke x. 19. Ps. xci. 3. saved—from every danger, from every
2 Pet. ii. 9. snare, from every temptation, from
2 Sam. iii. 18. "the hand of *all* our enemies," from
Tit. ii. 14. our sins? In death we would cling to
1 Tim. i. 15. the words, "Christ Jesus came into the world to save sinners.' Why

not in life equally cling to, and equally make real use of, the promise, "He shall save His people from their sins"— Matt. i. 21.
not merely from sin in general, but definitely "from *their* sins," personal and plural sins? "Is My hand shortened at all that it can not redeem? or have I no power to deliver?" Isa. l. 2.

His salvation is indeed finished, His work is perfect; and yet our King is still "working salvation in the midst of the earth," applying the reality of His salvation (if we will only believe His power) to the daily details of our pilgrimage and our warfare. We need it not only at last, but now—every hour, every minute. And the King "shall deliver the needy when he crieth," "and shall save the souls of the needy." John xvii. 4. Deut. xxxii. 4. Ps. lxxiv. 12. Ib. lxxii. 12. Ib. lxxii. 13.

May He say to your soul this day "I am *thy* salvation." Ib. xxxv. 3.

Look away to Jesus, Heb. xii. 2.
  Look away from all! Ps. cxxi. 1-3.
Then we need not stumble, Prov. iii. 23.

Prov. iv. 12.
Jude 24.
Ps. xxv. 15.
Luke x. 19.
1 Sam. xxii. 23.
Ps. xxxiv. 5, 6.

Then we shall not fall.
From each snare that lureth,
Foe or phantom grim,
Safety this ensureth,
Look away to Him!

THIRTIETH DAY.

Good Tidings to the King's Household.

"We do not well: this day is a day of 2 Kings vii. 9.
good tidings, and we hold our peace; if
we tarry till the morning light, some mischief will
come upon us; now, therefore, come, that we may go
and tell the king's household."

JUST the last persons who would seem to
need "good tidings," and the Ib. vii. 3.
last, too, who would seem likely to
have them to convey! But oh, how true the
figure is! how many among the King's own
household need the good tidings which these
lepers brought! For they are starv- Ps. lxxxi. 10-16.
ing so near to plenty, and poor 1 Cor. iii. 21,
within reach of treasure, and think- 22.
ing themselves besieged when the Lord has
dispersed the foe for them Is it Heb. ii. 14,
not often the spiritual leper, the 15.
conscious outcast, the famine-stricken, posses-

sionless soul, who takes the boldest step into the fullest salvation, and finds deliverance and abundance and riches beyond what the more favored and older inmate of the
1 Cor. ii. 12. King's household knows anything about?

2 Cor. ii. 11. It may be one of the enemy's devices, that we sometimes hold back good tidings, just because we shrink from telling them to the King's household. How many who do not hesitate to speak of Jesus to little children or poor people, or even to persons
Luke xix. 14. who openly say, "We will not have this man to reign over us," never say one word to their fellow-subjects about the
John xvi. 14, 15. blessed discoveries that the Holy Spirit has made to them of the fullness of His salvation, and the reality of His power, and the treasures of His word, and the satisfaction of His love, and the far-reaching fulfillments of His promises, and the real, actual deliverance, and freedom, and victory,
Rom. viii. 37. which He gives, and the strength
Acts iii. 16. and the healing that flow through faith in His name!

Satan even perverts humility into a hinderance in this, and persuades us that of course our friend knows as much or more of this than we do, and that telling of what we have found in Jesus, may seem like or lead to talking about ourselves. Yet perhaps all the while that friend is hungering and feeling besieged, while we are withholding good tidings of plenty and deliverance. Verily, "we do not well." Have there not been days when the brightest of us would have been most thankful for the simplest word about Jesus from the humblest Christian—days when even "the mention of His name" might have been food and freedom!

Prov. xi. 24-26.

James iv. 17.

It does not in the least follow that members of Christian families need no such "good tidings" because of their favored position. They may need it all the more, because no one thinks it necessary to try and help *them.* "As we have therefore opportunity, let us do good unto *all* men, specially unto them who are of the household of faith."

Gal. vi. 10

And when? The constantly-recurring word meets us here again, "*Now!*"

THIRTY-FIRST DAY.

The Prosperity of the King.

Jer. xxiii. 5. "A King shall reign and prosper."

IF we are really interested, heart and soul, in a person, how delighted we are to have positive assurance of his prosperity, and how extremely interested and pleased we feel at hearing anything about it! Is not this a test of our love to our King? Are we both interested and happy in the short, grand, positive words which are given us about His certain prosperity? If so, the pulse of our gladness is
Ps. xxxv. 27. beating true to the very heart of God,
Cf. Isa. lii. 13 (mar.) and liii. 10. for "Jehovah hath pleasure in the prosperity of His servant."

His prosperity is both absolute and increasing. Even now, "Thy wisdom and
1 Kings x. 7. prosperity exceedeth the fame that I heard." If we could get one glimpse of our

King in His present glory and joy, how we who love Him would rejoice for Him and with Him! And if we could get one great view of the wide, but hidden prosperity of His kingdom *at this moment*, where would be our discouragement and faint-heartedness! Suppose we could see how His work is going on in every soul that He has redeemed out of every kindred and tongue all over the world, with the same distinctness with which we see it in the last trophy of His grace for which we have been praising Him, would it not be a revelation of entirely overwhelming joy? Many Christians nowadays are foregoing an immense amount of cheer, because they do not take the trouble to inquire, or read, or go where they can hear about the present prosperity of His kingdom. Those who do not care much, can hardly be loving much or helping much.

1 Pet. iii. 22.

Rev. v. 9.

But we *do* care about it; and so how jubilantly the promises of His *increasing* prosperity ring out to *us!* "He *must* increase." "He *must* reign, till He hath put all enemies under His feet." "Of the

John iii. 30.

1 Cor. xv. 25

Isa. ix. 7.

increase of His government and peace there shall be *no* end."

All our natural delight in progress finds satisfaction here—no stagnation, no reaching a dead level; we are on an ever-winning side, bound up with an ever-progressing cause. A typical light on this point flashes from the story of
2 Sam. v. 10. David. He "went on and grew great," or, as the margin has it, "going and growing;" which we can not forbear connecting with the promise to ourselves, "Ye
Mal. iv. 2. shall *go* forth and *grow* up." And
1 Chron. xi. 9. then we are told that he "waxed greater and greater" (marg.), "went on going and *increasing*."

But we must not be merely onlookers. Let us see to it, first, that there be increasing prosperity in His kingdom in our hearts. Pray that He may not only reign, but prosper in that domain. And next, let us see to it that we are doing all we can to further His prosperity all around us. Translate our daily prayer, "Thy
Matt. vi. 10. kingdom come," into daily, burning, glowing action for its prosperity.

FIRST SUNDAY.

The Table of the King.

"As for Mephibosheth, said the king, he shall eat at my table, as one of the king's sons." 2 Sam. ix. 11.

IN every thought connected with the King's table we see Jesus only.

He prepares the feast—"Thou Ps. xxiii. 5.
preparest a table before me." He
gives the invitation—"Come thou 2 Sam. xix.
over with me, and I will feed thee 33.
with me." He gives the qualifying position of
adoption, receiving us as "the King's Gal. iv. 5
sons." He brings us into "His ban- Cant. ii. 4.
queting-house." He bids us partake, saying,
"Eat, O friends· drink, yea, drink Ib. v. 1.
abundantly, O beloved." He is with
us at the feast, for "the King sitteth Ib. i. 12.

at His table." He Himself is the heavenly food, the bread and the meat of His table; for
John vi. 51. He says, "The bread that I will
Ib. vi. 55. give is My flesh," and "My flesh is meat indeed."

He Himself! Nothing less is offered to us, for nothing less could truly satisfy. How wonderfully the spiritual feeding, with its mode and its means, is expressed in the words of our Communion Service: "Feed on Him in thy heart by faith, with thanksgiving." "Feed *on Him!*"—not on sacred emblem, not on "outward and visible sign," but on Himself. This *first*
John vi. 57. in place, first in thought. "He that eateth *Me*" (can words be stronger?), "even he shall live by Me." Then the mode, "*in thy heart;*" then the means, "*by faith*"—could it close otherwise than "*with thanksgiving?*"

It is not occasional, but continual feeding on
Ps. cvii. 9. Christ that really satisfies the long-
2 Sam. ix 13. ing soul, and fills the hungry soul with goodness. "He did eat *continually* at the king's table." It is "he that
John vi. 35. *cometh* to Me" who "shall never

hunger," not "he who did come." 1 Pet. ii. 4.
"To whom *coming*," always coming, never going away, because we "have Ib. ii. 3.
tasted that the Lord is gracious," we shall be "built up." Ib. ii. 5.

If we are really guests at the King's table in its fullest sense—if we are feeding upon Christ Himself, and not on any shadow of the true substance—we must be satisfied. Here is a strong, severe test. Christ *must* satisfy; then, if we are not satisfied, it must be because we are not feeding on Him wholly and only. The fault is not in the provision which is made—"For all that came unto King Solomon's table, they lacked nothing." 1 Kings iv. 27.

When we feel that "we are not worthy so much as to gather up the crumbs under His table," how precious are the words, "This man receiveth sinners, and eateth with them!" Luke xv. 2. When we remember that we were dead in trespasses and sins, Eph. ii. 1. we may recollect that Lazarus, the raised one, "was one of them that sat at the table with Him." John xii. 2. When we come back from the battle-field, weary, yet victorious,

Heb. vii. 2. we may look for our King of Peace
Gen. xiv. 18. coming to meet us with bread and wine and His own priestly blessing, that we may be strengthened and refreshed by Himself.

SECOND SUNDAY.

Listening for the King's Voice.

"Let my lord the king now speak." 2 Sam. xiv 18.

ARE we not apt to think more of speaking to the King than of the King speaking to us? We come to the throne of grace with the glad and solemn purpose, "I will now speak unto the King." And we pour out our hearts before Him, and tell Him all the sins and all the needs, all the joys and all the sorrows, till the very telling seems almost an answer, because it brings such a sense of relief. It is very sweet, very comforting to do this.

2 Sam. xiv. 15. Ps. lxii. 8. 1 Kings x. 2. Mark vi. 30.

But this is only half-communion; and we miss, perhaps, a great deal of unknown blessing by being content with this one-sided audience.

We should use another "*now*," and say, "Let my lord the King now speak." We expect Him to speak sometime, but not actually and literally "now," while we kneel before Him. And therefore we do not listen, and

Luke vii. 40. therefore we do not hear what He has to say to us.

What about last time we knelt in prayer? Surely He had more to say to us than we had to say to Him, and yet we never waited a minute to see! We did not give Him opportunity for His gracious response. We rushed away from our King's presence as soon as we had said our say, and vaguely expected Him to send His answers after us somehow and sometime, but not there and then. What wonder if they have not yet reached us! The only wonder is that He ever speaks at all when we

Ib. x. 39. act thus. If Mary had talked to the Lord Jesus all the time she sat at His feet, she would not have "heard His word." But is not this pretty much what we have done?

Not that we should pray less, but listen more. And the more we listen, the more we shall want to say afterward. "Thou shalt call, and I will answer." (Job xiii. 22.) But we may miss the sweetest whispers of His love by not saying, "Speak, Lord," (1 Sam. iii. 9.) and not hushing ourselves to "*hear* what God the Lord will speak." (Ps. lxxxv. 8.) We can not hear His "still, small voice" (1 Kings xix. 12.) during a torrent of noisy, and impatient, and hurried petition. "I will watch to see what He will say unto me." (Hab. ii. 1.)

We must "let the King now speak;" not our own hearts and our wandering thoughts, not the world and not the tempter—we must not *let* these speak; they must be silenced with holy determination. And we must let the King speak *as* King, meeting His utterance with implicit submission and faith and obedience; receiving His least hint with total homage, and love, and gratitude.

He has many a blessed surprise for us in thus listening. We may come very diffidently saying, "Let thine handmaid, I pray thee, speak *one word* unto my (2 Sam. xiv. 12.)

lord the King," and, having said it, *wait*, saying, "Let my Lord the King *now* speak," and
John xvi. 12. then find that He has *many things* to
say "to us."

He will be speaking to many this day in His
Isa. l. 4. house of prayer. He will "know
how to speak a word in season" to
Hos. ii. 14. see marg. each listening heart; He will
"speak comfortably." And His peo-
Isa. lii. 6. ple shall know that it is "He that
doth speak." Then let our prayer
Cant. viii. 13. be, "The companions hearken to
Thy voice; cause *me* to hear it!"

Our own belovèd Master "hath many things to say;
Look forward to His teaching, unfolding day by day
To whispers of His Spirit, while resting at His feet,
To glowing revelation, to insight clear and sweet.

THIRD SUNDAY.

Seeing the King.

"Go forth, O ye daughters of Zion, and Cant. iii. 11.
behold King Solomon."

PERHAPS we have dwelt more upon the
promise, "Thine eyes shall see Isa. xxxiii.
the King in His beauty," than upon 17.
the command, "Go forth and behold" Him.
We are not to be content with languidly saying, "We would see Jesus." If our John xii. 21
eyes are too dim, let us pray, "Open Ps. cxix. 18.
Thou mine eyes;" if there is a veil upon our
hearts, let us turn to the Lord the Spirit, and
"it shall be taken away;" if we are 1 Cor. iii. 16.
standing too far off to see, let us utter
the cry and the resolve, "Draw me, Cant. i. 4.
we will run after Thee;" if we are sitting still
in the house, let us arise quickly and John xi. 20,
go to meet Jesus. 29.

This is neither an impossible nor a delusive command. The eye that looks away up to Jesus
Heb. xii. 2. *will* behold Him now. And what shall we behold? The vision is all of beauty and glory and coronation now. The sor-
Isa. lii. 14. row and the marred visage are past; and even when we behold Him as
Rev. v. 6. the Lamb of God, it is the Lamb "in the midst of the throne" *now*.

O daughters of Zion, who gaze by faith upon Jesus our King, what do you see? Oh, the
Heb. ii. 9. music of the answers!—"We see
Ps. xlv. 2. Jesus crowned with glory and honor!" "Fairer than the children
Isa. iv. 2. of men!" "Beautiful and glorious!"
Zech. ix. 17. "How great is His beauty!" "His
Cant. v. 15. countenance is as Lebanon, excel-
Rev. i. 16. lent as the cedars," and "as the sun
Cant. v. 16. shineth in his strength!" "Yea, He is altogether lovely!"

When we have seen the beauty of our King once, we want to see it always. Then, not till then, we really do not care for any other sight, except in so far as it reflects or illustrates what we see in Him; then, not till then, we can say,

"*One* thing have I desired of the Lord, that will I seek after; that I may dwell in the house of the Lord all the days of my life, to behold the beauty of the Lord." (Ps. xxvii. 4.) And when we can honestly say, "*One* thing," then, as has been tellingly said, "life is wonderfully simplified."

Conversely, it is not till we do say, "*One* thing," that the desire is fulfilled, and we "see His face with joy." (Job. xxxiii. 26.) How *can* we "see His face" when we are straining our eyes to see all sorts of other things!

A true sight of the King will give a terrible sight of our own uncleanness and deformity; but the altar-fire shall touch our lips, the iniquity shall be taken away and the sin purged, (Isa. vi. 6, 7.) and then "the beauty of the Lord our God shall be upon us," (Ps. xc. 17.) for "we all, beholding with open face as in a glass the glory of the Lord, are (not even shall be, but *are*) changed into the same image, from glory to glory." (2 Cor. iii. 18.)

Lord Jesus, enable us to 'go forth and behold Thee" this day; fulfill Thy promise that

John xiv. 21. Thou wilt manifest Thyself to those who love Thee; and grant us this day to see Thy beauty, Thy power, Ps. lxiii. 2. and Thy glory, yea, Thyself, in Thy sanctuary!

From glory unto glory! Our faith hath seen the
King;
We own His matchless beauty, as adoringly we sing;
But He hath more to show us! O thought of untold
bliss!
And we press on exultingly in certain hope to this:—

To marvelous outpourings of His treasures new and
old,
To largess of His bounty paid in the King's own
gold,
To glorious expansion of His mysteries of grace,
To radiant unveilings of the brightness of His face.

FOURTH SUNDAY.

Coming to the King.

2 Chron. ix. 1–12.

I.

I CAME from very far away, to see
The King of Salem; for I had been told
Of glory and of wisdom manifold,
And condescension infinite and free.
How could I rest when I had heard His fame
In that dark, lonely land of death from whence
I came?

II.

I came (but not like Sheba's Queen) alone!
No stately train, no costly gifts to bring;
No friend at court, save One, that One the
King!

I had requests to spread before His throne,
And I had questions none could solve for me
Of import deep, and full of awful mystery.

III.

I came and communed with that mighty King,
  And told Him all my heart; I can not say
  In mortal ear what communings were they.
But wouldst thou know, go too, and meekly
    bring
All that is in thy heart, and thou shalt hear
His voice of love and power, His answers
    sweet and clear.

IV.

Oh, happy end of every weary quest!
  He told me all I needed, graciously—
  Enough for guidance, and for victory
O'er doubts and fears, enough for quiet rest;
And when some veiled response I could not
    read,
It was not hid from Him—this was enough
    indeed.

V.

His wisdom and His glories passed before
  My wondering eyes in gradual revelation;
  The house that He had built, its strong foundation,
Its living stones, and, brightening more and more,
Fair glimpses of that palace far away,
Where all His loyal ones shall dwell with Him for aye.

VI.

True, the report that reached my far-off land
  Of all His wisdom and transcendent fame;
  Yet I believèd not until I came—
Bowed to the dust, till raised by royal hand.
The half was never told by mortal word:
My King exceeded all the fame that I had heard!

VII.

Oh, happy are His servants! happy they
  Who stand continually before His face,
  Ready to do His will of wisest grace!

My King! is mine such blessedness to-day?
For I, too, hear Thy wisdom, line by line
Thy ever brightening words in holy radiance
shine.

VIII.

Oh, blessed be the Lord thy God, who set
Our King upon His throne! divine delight
In the Belovèd, crowning Thee with might,
Honor and majesty supreme; and yet
The strange and God-like secret opening
thus—
The Kingship of His Christ ordained through
love to us!

IX.

What shall I render to my glorious King?
I have but that which I receive from Thee,
And what I give Thou givest back to me,
Transmuted by Thy touch; each worthless
thing
Changed to the preciousness of gem or gold,
And by Thy blessing multiplied a thousand-
fold.

X.

All my desire Thou grantest, whatsoe'er
I ask! Was ever mythic tale or dream
So bold as this reality—this stream
Of boundless blessings flowing full and free?
Yet more than I have thought or asked of Thee,
Out of Thy royal bounty still Thou givest me!

XI.

Now will I turn to mine own land, and tell
What I myself have seen and heard of Thee,
And give Thine own sweet message, "Come and see!"
And yet in heart and mind forever dwell
With Thee, my King of Peace, in loyal rest,
Within the fair pavilion of Thy presence blest.

"Surely in what place my Lord the King shall be whether in death or life, even there also will thy servant be."—2 SAM. xv. 15.

"Where I am, there shall also my servant be."—JOHN xii. 26.

FIFTH SUNDAY.

The Coming of the King.

"Behold, He cometh."—Rev. i. 7.

I.

THOU art coming, O my Saviour!
  Thou art coming, O my King!
In Thy beauty all-resplendent,
In Thy glory all-transcendent;
  Well may we rejoice and sing!
Coming! In the opening east,
  Herald brightness slowly swells;
Coming! O my glorious Priest,
  Hear we not Thy golden bells?

II.

Thou art coming, Thou art coming!
  We shall meet Thee on Thy way;
We shall see Thee, we shall know Thee,
We shall bless Thee, we shall show Thee

All our hearts could never say!
What an anthem that will be,
Ringing out our love to Thee,
Pouring out our rapture sweet
At Thine own all-glorious feet!

III.

Thou art coming! Rays of glory,
Through the veil Thy death has rent
Touch the mountain and the river
With a golden glowing quiver,
Thrill of light and music blent.
Earth is brightened when this gleam
Falls on flower and rock and stream;
Life is brightened when this ray
Falls upon its darkest day.

IV.

Not a cloud and not a shadow,
Not a mist and not a tear,
Not a sin and not a sorrow,
Not a dim and veiled to-morrow,
For that sunrise grand and clear!
Jesus, Saviour, once with Thee,

Nothing else seems worth a thought!
Oh, how marvelous will be
All the bliss Thy pain hath bought!

V.

Thou art coming! At Thy table
We are witnesses for this,
While remembering hearts Thou meetest,
In communion clearest, sweetest,
Earnest of our coming bliss;
Showing not Thy death alone,
And Thy love exceeding great,
But Thy coming and Thy throne,
All for which we long and wait.

VI.

Thou art coming! We are waiting
With a hope that can not fail,
Asking not the day or hour,
Resting on Thy word of power,
Anchored safe within the veil.
Time appointed may be long,
But the vision must be sure:
Certainty shall make us strong;
Joyful patience can endure.

VII.

Oh, the joy to see Thee reigning,
  Thee, my own belovèd Lord!
Every tongue Thy name confessing,
Worship, honor, glory, blessing,
  Brought to Thee with glad accord!
Thee, my Master and my Friend,
  Vindicated and enthroned!
Unto earth's remotest end
  Glorified, adored, and owned!

www.ingramcontent.com/pod-product-compliance
Lightning Source LLC
LaVergne TN
LVHW021412110826
845150LV00007B/1884